A family view — ★ ★ ★ ★ ★

"I must confess that this is my favorite story these days. Joe Fortenberry is my father and Beth Fortenberry is my cousin. She has caught the spirit and essence of the Olympic tale as told to me by my Pop. This is a mixture of old-fashioned American sport against the spectre of Nazi Germany. Beth weaves an entertaining story, from the advent of basketball to the first Gold Medal. I know the story probably as well as anyone, and yet I felt as though I was discovering this lost gem of a tale for the first time. I envy those who will read it for the first time. I highly recommend this tale of the Depression, the Dust Bowl, Nazis, basketball, and good versus evil. Sounds like a good premise for a Spielberg movie."

Oliver Fortenberry—November 5, 2019

True Champions — ★ ★ ★ ★ ★

"This book reads just like the description—a play-by-play sports news show with high energy, moving inspiration, and mind-blowing challenges that our first-ever US basketball team overcame to win the gold medal at the summer Olympics in Berlin during the Hitler era! This incredible book illustrates how our very first basketball team and how the first-ever slam dunk went down in history. This will definitely be an exciting film to watch on the big screen!"

Cali Rossen, Best-Selling Author, Actress—October 31, 2019

Much, much more than hoops — ★ ★ ★ ★ ★

Fortenberry stays true to the incredible story that begins with James Naismith meeting his wife and saving his career by inventing the great sport of basketball (all in one week). The book traces basketball's evolution from the first game in 1891 through the 1936 Olympics, where Team USA won the sport's first gold medal. There are stars galore, as the story reveals the interactions of Naismith (as inventor), Phog Allen (as father of basketball coaching), and John McLendon (father of basketball integration). *Slam Dunk* is much more than a sports story and delivers a unique perspective on early twentieth century Americana, the Great Depression, and the 1936 Nazi Olympics.

Rich Hughes, Author, Netting Out Basketball 1936:
The Remarkable Story of the McPherson Refiners,
the First Team to Dunk, Zone Press, and Win
the Olympic Gold Medal—*November 5, 2019*

Mind, body, spirit—combining education, sports, and spirituality and this book! — ★ ★ ★ ★ ★

Los Angeles author Beth Fortenberry makes a sparkling literary debut with *SLAM DUNK*—a book that is already in the process of becoming a movie. Beth is a writer-producer and a member of Actors Equity, Screen Actors Guild, and the Academy of Television Arts and Sciences. Of interest, she also worked as a Playboy Bunny in New York in the past! She brings to this interesting book a sound journalistic mind, able to share sports in a manner that reads like a novel.

For example, Beth states "Ever wondered who invented basketball or who invented the slam dunk? Well, I can clear that up for you. James Naismith invented basketball and Joe Fortenberry invented the dunk. Yep, Joe is my cousin, and I grew up thinking everyone had a 6′8″ relative with an Olympic gold medal that he kept in a shoebox, on the high shelf in the hall closet! Seven years ago, when Joe's children decided this would make a good movie, I was summoned, and it's my pleasure to share this story with you."

This well-written account of the history of basketball, now a favorite US sport, proceeds from how it developed from the initial idea in 1891 (including the 13 Rules of Basketball), through the myriad aspects of its growth, including the many players and others who shaped its development through World War I and the Dust Bowl, and up through the 1936 "Hitler" Olympics. It is not only a fascinating history exploration, but also a fine homage to the many people who made the sport important—and memorable! For sports fans, this book is a *must* read, and for fans of fine writing, meet the remarkable Beth Fortenberry. Recommend

Grady Harp, Hall of Fame Top 100 Reviewer—November 2, 2019

Fascinating history — ★ ★ ★ ★

Beth Fortenberry writes a fascinating book about how basketball was invented in *SLAM DUNK: The True Story of Basketball's First Olympic Gold Medal Team*. The author first gives the highlights of James Naismith's life and what caused him to invent the indoor game. You would also appreciate the sweet way he met and dated his wife. Then we are introduced to Joe Fortenberry. His skill and love for basketball take him to great challenges and victories.

SLAM DUNK, by Beth Fortenberry, is told in a way that brings basketball, James Naismith, and Joe Fortenberry alive. A motion picture is in the making, featuring this book. I loved the book because I can now talk more intelligently with my teenage sons. I am looking forward to them reading this book also; they will love it. The history surrounding the Olympics is amazing, as Hitler has his part in this book.

JoJo Maxson—November 3, 2019

Well written — ★ ★ ★ ★ ★

The book is written very well, looks like a lot of research done, made for a great book.

Debra Powell—November 4, 2019

Interesting for all; a must read
for sports enthusiasts — ★ ★ ★ ★ ★

The author has provided a gold mine for readers interested in the historical background of sports. Not only has she disclosed little-known facts about the origin of basketball and details of the players involved in these early endeavors—Fortenberry, "Tex" Gibbons, ball hawk Francis Johnson, Sam Balter, one of the Jews on the 1936 Olympic team, and others—but she has included largely unknown or often overlooked features of prominent people associated with the Olympics and other sports; e.g., Coach Jimmy Needles; Phog Allen; Gene Johnson; the mercurial Olympic politician Avery Brundage; and Maude Sherman Naismith, organizer of the first women's basketball team as well as earlier having devised the first usable football helmet, noted by Amos Alonzo Stagg (the legendary football player/coach long associated with the Y.M.C.A.). The description of Hitler's and Goebbels' activities and that of the German people of the era are most appropriately portrayed. In all, this is an interesting book and a must read for sport aficionados.

John Manhold—November 4, 2019

"The best basketball story since *Hoosiers* and destined to be a major motion picture."
—Carter DeHaven, producer of *Hoosiers*

SLAM DUNK

Joe Fortenberry "dunking"—1936 Olympics

SLAM DUNK

THE TRUE STORY OF BASKETBALL'S
FIRST OLYMPIC GOLD MEDAL TEAM

BY

BETH FORTENBERRY

HybridGlobal
PUBLISHING

Published by
Hybrid Global Publishing
301 E 57th Street, 4th fl
New York, NY 10022

Manufactured in the United States of America, or in the United Kingdom when distributed elsewhere.

Fortenberry, Beth
SLAM DUNK:
The True Story of Basketball's First Olympic Gold Medal Team
LCCN: 2019916780
ISBN: 978-1-948181-91-4
eBook: 978-1-948181-92-1

Cover design by: Jenici Fortenberry Reid
Photos credits: Headshot, Michael Higgins
Interior design: Medlar Publishing Solutions Pvt Ltd., India
Permission credits: Joe Fortenberry Estate, Public Domain

www.BethFortenberry.com

Disclaimer:
This is a work of narrative non-fiction. Certain situations were condensed or arranged for dramatic effect.

DEDICATION

For my husband, Steven
And my children—Jacob, Adam, Sydney, and Daniel

TABLE OF CONTENTS

Foreword . . . . *xv*

Acknowledgments . . . . *xvii*

Prologue . . . . *xix*

1. Love at First Sight 1

2. The Incorrigibles and the Invention of Basketball 3

3. More About Maude 17

4. "Quig" Quigley and "Phog" Allen 23

5. Joe Fortenberry 29

6. Phog and the 1932 Olympics 33

7. Gas and Gold 37

8. The Olympics and John McLendon 39

9. The Swimming Pool and Kansas University 1933 41

10. Coach Gene Johnson 45

11. Hitler and Leni, Laemmle and Frankenstein 49

12. Joe Fortenberry—Home Away From Home 55

13. Phog, Maude, and the Universals 59

14. Avery Brundage and the Berlin Connection 63

15. Reality 69

16. Hitler vs. Jews, Blacks, and Women. 73

17. Pride and the Slam Dunk. 111

18. About Maude. 119

19. The A.A.U. Finals. 121

20. No Money for the Olympics 125

21. The Invitation 133

22. Even More Problems 141

23. On the Way to Berlin 149

24. The *S.S. Manhattan* 155

25. The Olympic Village. 161

26. The Unbelievable New Rules 165

27. The Opening Ceremony 169

28. Hitler and Jesse Owens 173

29. Down to Business 177

30. Home. 187

Epilogue. 189

Whatever Happened to... 191

Bibliography 195

About the Author 199

FOREWORD

You've got to understand that I receive over sixty scripts a year, not to mention books and articles about basketball. I've read almost every basketball story that's ever been brought to Hollywood's attention. That's what I get for producing *Hoosiers*, the movie that many consider to be the best basketball movie ever made. Most often, when I start reading, I don't even get past the first page.

When *SLAM DUNK—The True Story of Basketball's First Olympic Gold Medal Team* came my way, I immediately knew this was something very special. I read it from beginning to end in one sitting. The content, the story, the unknown historical facts, the tragedies, the writing, the interesting characters, the very special young athletes, the unbelievable odds, the writer's ability to combine the story from 1891 with later pivotal events, such as World War 1, the Dust Bowl, and the 1936 "Hitler" Olympics, make this an epic story. I knew this story was very special, and I'm lucky to be involved. From the players to the writer, this is the real deal.

Carter DeHaven, Producer
Los Angeles, 2019

ACKNOWLEDGMENTS

One day, out of the blue, my cousin Sally called and wanted to know if I would be interested in making a movie about her dad, Joe Fortenberry. I grew up thinking everyone had a 6′8″ relative who kept an Olympic gold medal for basketball in the hall closet on the high shelf, way at the back. Naturally, I was intrigued. Seven years later, I'm happy to report that this has been the ride of a lifetime and there are many people to thank:

Dan and Sally Fortenberry Nibbelink
Oliver Fortenberry
Kirk and Trish Fortenberry Hill
Taylor and Jenici Fortenberry Reid
Connie Schmidt Schweer
Jerry Johnson
Beverly and Jim Naismith
Naismith Memorial Basketball Hall of Fame
Nancy and Rich Hughes
Carter DeHaven
The 1936 Olympic gold medal team

The entire Fortenberry family, Terry and Claire Fortenberry Mepham, Ann Hancock, Mark Hancock, Jack and Cyn Fortenberry Hall, Rita Fortenberry, Joann and Jim Rimpau, Bonnie and Phil Hancock, Ramona Hammer, Leisa Fortenberry, Sally and Jim Fortenberry, Monica Fortenberry Higdon, Becky Ford Fortenberry, Steve and Sherry Maysonave, Jon Mark Beilue, Brett Whitenack, Ann Hassler, Jeff Pirtle, Jeff Thompson, Michelle Fandetti, Sharkie Zartman, Darlene and Ken Tipton, Nancy Sandoval, Rick Young, Beverly Ansara, Suzzy Canny, Valerie Klein, Sally Wilk, Joe Bates, Howard Canode Trisha Dunn, Sharon Killoran, Debra Powell, Michael Park, Kevin Connelly, Bonnie and Barry Goldstein, Todd Resnick, Jay Balaban, Barry Fleet, Sean Cunningham, Barry Kritz, Nancy and Mark Aston, Ken Zakin, Michael Chesner, Dave Wilczynski, Harvey Berkowitz, Johnie Burkhalter and the Tascosa Rebels!, Alyssa Woodall, Wayne "Slap" Slappy, Billy Blanks, David Tannenbaum, Russ Miceli, Steven Tannenbaum, Jacob LeGrant, Adam LeGrant, Christopher Belt, Sydney Tannenbaum, Matt Zeysing, John DoLeva, Marilyn McNicolas and the Bonelli family, Julie DeHaven, Cali and Chris Rossen, Pam Putnam Whitaker, Michael Higgins, Sheri Sasaki, Ingrid Scott, Peter Shustari, Sheila Tanenbaum, Jean Thornton, Steve Harrison and the National Publicity Summit—particularly Deb Englander, Ginny Shepard, Alex Carroll, and Gail Snyder—the Tannenbaum Family, the Lobel Family, the Van Houten Family, Alan Watt, Viki King, Natasha and Craig Duswalt, Karen Strauss, Sara Foley and Sundar.

Special thanks to Ed Wright.

PROLOGUE

There's running on a shiny, maple basketball court. Heavy breathing is so intense, it's almost like hearing sweat. Sneakers squeak. Then, whoosh, the ball shimmies through the basket. A crowd jumps to its feet. The applauding and cheering make all the hard work and years of practice worth every second. James Naismith, the inventor of basketball, would be very proud. This is his story.

It was one of those perfect fall evenings on Saturday, September 8, 1979, for induction night at the Naismith Memorial Basketball Hall of Fame in Springfield, Massachusetts. Springfield is where basketball was born, and now gleaming black stretch limousines arrive in organized order. Drivers open limo doors to release the inductees of 1979 and their families: coach Sam Barry, player Wilt Chamberlain, the famous commentator James Enright, coach Edgar Hickey, coach John McLendon, coach Ray Meyer, and coach Pete Newell. Other towering basketball stars are surrounded by photographers, reporters, and TV cameras. It's like being in the Land of the Tall. In this world, everyone, including the staff, is fit, athletic, and on top of their game.

In the auditorium, the Father of Basketball Integration, Coach John McLendon, now age 64, stands at the podium and gently clears his throat to begin his speech. "Yes, I coached three national championship teams, and yes, I helped integrate basketball. But the credit goes to my parents and my mentor, the man himself, James Naismith. It's with great pride and humility that I share with you about the Canadian-American who invented basketball, saved his job, and met his wife—all in the same week."

CHAPTER 1

LOVE AT FIRST SIGHT

Greetings from a freezing, yet sunny day in late December, 1891. Picture-perfect snow sparkles on the grounds and buildings, and in the trees. Bundled-up children are laughing with pent-up abandon as they shovel snow from the steps of the Y.M.C.A. (Young Men's Christian Association). The building is quite grand. Red brick with white trim and the bronze Y.M.C.A. triangle with the inscription "Mind, Body, Spirit" emblazoned near the oversized wooden front doors.

Pretty, blue-eyed Southerner Maude Sherman, a teacher, shovels snow with her schoolchildren. Y.M.C.A. football coach Amos Stagg, a theological scholar turned All-American football player at Yale, walks with James Naismith, a 5'10" husky rugby type, who just turned 29 years old last month. Naismith has a handlebar mustache and an extra twinkle in his eye.

Amos waves and calls, "Hi, Maude. Did you get my thank-you note?"

As she turns, the sun glistens on her face and she seems to glow. She's so beautiful, it's almost spiritual. Naismith stops in his tracks.

Maude stops shoveling and says, "Yes, Amos, I did! How's the helmet working out?"

"The men love it. There's a lot less injuries. I can't thank you enough."

Maude's eyes venture toward Naismith. Amos quickly remembers his manners and says, "Oh, this is our latest faculty member, Dr. James Naismith. His degree is in theology."

Maude, who has been gazing a bit too long adds, "Nice to meet you." Naismith nods respectfully, then timidly looks into her eyes.

"Maude invented and sewed the first football helmet," Amos adds.

Naismith quips, "A helmet? Less injuries equals more wins. That's a very good idea."

Maude jokes, "I guess you could call me the Betsy Ross of football!"

The men laugh with her and Amos remarks, "Well, Betsy Ross might have designed the American flag but you, Maude Sherman, have saved many an injury."

Naismith asks, "Why are you shoveling snow?"

Maude replies, "We're clearing a path for others."

"Ah, a fine spiritual practice."

A rosy-cheeked little girl tugs on Maude's skirt and points to a snow pile.

"Miss Sherman, come look at our work," she says.

As the child tugs, Maude follows. Amos turns and starts walking with Naismith.

"Promise to visit us soon," Amos calls back to Maude.

Maude answers, "Promise." Then she adds, "Mind, Body, Spirit!"

The men reply, "Mind, Body, Spirit" as they walk toward the Y.M.C.A.

CHAPTER 2

THE INCORRIGIBLES AND THE INVENTION OF BASKETBALL

Later that day, in the well-equipped Y.M.C.A. gymnasium, eighteen postgraduate college men in gray sweat suits practice soccer drills aimlessly. Some retire to the parallel bars and some start a round of calisthenics. Naismith paces restlessly on the sidelines.

His boss, Dr. Luther Gulick, has a major problem. His job is to prepare teachers-in-training so they can be instructors and coaches in Y.M.C.A.s throughout the world. As the son of a missionary in Hawaii and an athlete himself, he thoroughly embraced the idea of "Muscular Christians"—God-fearing men who were athletes. He also had an artistic flair and designed the Y's inverted triangle symbol that represents the slogan "Mind, Body, Spirit."

Now he watches through a glass window as the mustached and bearded men goof off. To Naismith, the surprising thing about Gulick was that most of his professors at McGill University in Montreal, Canada, were elderly and stuffy. Luther Gulick was just a few years older than Naismith. He was tall, athletic, and buoyant, with red hair, a stylish mustache and piercing blue eyes. He was more like a clothes model than a Doctor of Education. But Naismith was soon to find out that he had a quick temper and the will to win at all costs, and that he was the type that would hire and fire until he gets what he wants.

"Naismith!" orders Gulick as he points toward the hall.

Naismith rushes toward Gulick and nervously exits with him through the side door. They walk down the hall at a swift pace.

"Yes, sir," Naismith replies.

"What's going on? I hired your Canadian-American, preaching backside because I've seen you do some of the meanest things in sports. But, in a most gentlemanly manner. Your job is to find a new game to keep our men in shape between the football and baseball seasons!"

"Yes! We've tried variations of rugby, soccer, and even lacrosse. Now, I think I have it."

"Combining education, sports, and spirituality is what the Y.M.C.A. is all about. This will lead to a deeper human understanding. We're committed to the development of the whole man, Naismith. Even if they're incorrigible and think they can't be improved."

"That's why I'm here. I know I can do it. I will not fail."

"Your assignment is due this week. You must find a game for our future teachers that's easy to learn, can be played inside or out, day or night. Or you can go back to Canada!"

"Yes, sir," Naismith responds as Gulick storms off.

Determined, Naismith returns to the gym and blows his whistle. The men are led by Frank Mahan, a burly Irishman from North Carolina, who wears an All Stars football jersey. His buddies—swashbuckling, full-bearded Canadian T. D. Patton and the very proper William Chase—don't move.

Mahan quips to Naismith, "You can always go back to preachin'."

"Nay, Incorrigibles, I'm in charge here! I'm not going back to preaching and I'm not losing my job because of you. You may have gotten rid of the two other coaches, but not me!" he bellows. "See you Monday morning. 11:30 a.m. sharp. Mahan, after you change, come see me."

"Yes, sir," Mahan says as he and the others trot off to shower.

Naismith trudges up the narrow stairs that lead to his cramped office above the locker room. It has a small window overlooking the gym, and that window is the only source of light. Naismith quickly closes its curtain. In times like this, he starts to daydream. His mind returns to the dark hayloft on his uncle Peter's farm near Bennies Corners in Ontario. It was the only safe place he could cry his lonely tears and "talk" to his mother.

He never fully recovered from being orphaned at nine years old and always carried a burden of shame, wondering if his parents' deaths were somehow his fault. For the life in him, he couldn't understand how anyone could speak disrespectfully to a parent, especially a mother!

His father, John Naismith, arrived from Scotland on the eastern shores of Canada at 14 years old. He settled on his uncle's farm until he was 18. Then he went out on his own and started to work for a carpenter for a dollar a year. That apprenticeship paved the way for the fledgling entrepreneur to become a building contractor and to partner with fellow Scot, Robert Young. The business was successful and John wound up marrying Robert's sister, Margaret, in 1858. Her father gave them a piece of land nearby in Ramsey, Ontario, and John built a house for them on it.

The closest big town was Almonte, Ontario. Almonte was founded in the 1820s by religious, hard-working Scottish immigrants. The area had all the natural resources of home and lots of inexpensive rural farmland. By the mid-1800s more than 90,000 people had emigrated to Canada to pursue the occupations they had in Scotland. But in America and Canada they could provide a better life for themselves and their families. They were frugal and resourceful, and had a disciplined work ethic. There was always room for the next group of relatives and friends coming from Scotland on the next boat.

A typical evening would be around the fireplace with the women spinning their yarn, knitting, and sewing. The men would sharpen their tools and mend harnesses. Children sat with them and played with their toys. Everyone stayed for evening prayers.

The clan had a real sense of church, community, and family. There was always a church social or an election or a graduation to look forward to. Scottish leaders thrived and went on to make their world a better place. James McGill founded McGill University in 1813, and many ran for political office and won.

James (Jim) Naismith was born in Ramsey, Ontario, on his sister Annie's birthday, November 6, 1861. She was four years older and immediately took an interest in caring for baby Jim. Their little brother Robbie was born in 1866.

In America, the Civil War was raging, causing continental and transatlantic trade havoc as well as political tension. However, the Canadians wisely went on with their own business. When the war was over in 1865, it was a huge relief to Canada, which didn't want involvement with America's war. The return to normal trade provided the opportunity for John Naismith to build a series of badly needed houses in Almonte. John jumped at the chance, and the entire family moved at once.

Every summer Jim Naismith would go to stay at his Grandpa Young's farm. His grandfather was a cabinet maker and a farmer. Year after year, Jim looked forward to this visit. There, he learned lessons that would serve him throughout his life. One day, six-year-old-Jim and Grandpa were riding the buggy to see a client. Grandpa hitched the horses and told Jim to wait for him, as he would be only a few minutes. But Jim was not to touch the small pouch on the buggy seat.

Grandpa wasn't gone for one second before Jim starting eyeing that pouch. He picked it up and smelled it. Ummm. Chewing tobacco. Immediately he took a pinch. Grandpa watched and let the chew do its work. Soon Jim's head dropped and he was passing out. Grandpa hurried to the buggy and started home. The fresh air would bring the child back to life and, supposedly, the lesson would be learned.

No chewing tobacco or smoking of any kind was the lesson, but that didn't stop Jim from smoking from an old pipe that the teamsters would share with him when he was eight years old. He could smoke and cuss with the best of them. The teamsters were a rough lot, and Jim learned to be tough with them. He enjoyed being one of the men.

He met them when the family moved to Grand Calumet Island. His father bought a sawmill to provide his own lumber for his building projects—a smart move that saved time and money. Plus, it was a great training ground for the younger Naismith, as his father wanted him to take over the sawmill one day.

Still in the summer, he went to Grandpa Young's to learn cabinetry and farming. Once when he was in the field with Grandpa trimming a fence row, Grandpa had a scythe and Jim had a small sickle. Suddenly, a squirrel appeared and Jim threw down his sickle and went after the animal. He bagged it and started home with his grandfather. About halfway down the road Grandpa Young turned to him and said, "Where's the sickle?"

"I left it by the fence row," he said.

"I'm sorry, but I can't pay you for this week's work, because you lost a tool and it costs money, Laddie."

Jim held back his tears and spent the rest of the way home in complete misery. When they reached the barn, Grandpa pulled out the sickle from underneath his coat.

"I'll pay you half of what you earned today," he said. Jim let out an exalted sigh of relief. More for the tool than for the money.

"Thank you, Grandpa. It won't happen again. You have my word."

"Well, see that you keep your word. It's as good as gold. Your word is what people will come to rely on. If you keep it, people will trust you. If you are trusted, you will go far in life."

Alone in the dark, Naismith returns from the daydream of his past and slumps in his chair, elbows on the desk, head in his hands. He hears the men in the locker room laughing about him. It hurts. He knows he must keep his word to Dr. Gulick and come up with a game to be played between the football and baseball seasons. But what? There was no time to feel sorry for himself, but his thoughts drifted to the summer of 1870, when his whole life changed in a span of four months.

Grandpa Young died on July 17 at age 68. As the family was mourning, his father's sawmill burned to the ground in a nasty fire. If that wasn't enough, his father contracted the highly contagious typhoid fever while trying to figure out what happened at the sawmill. Epidemics were common in rural areas. There were few doctors and they had to travel from a long way. Sick people were isolated and well family members were forbidden to go near them for fear of an epidemic that could wipe out a majority of the population.

When William, Margaret's brother, heard of John's illness, he hitched up his horses and went to fetch his sister and her three children. Margaret refused to go with her brother but insisted that the children leave with him. She felt she must stay and take care of her husband. She gathered the children's clothing and their few possessions, and sent them off with Uncle William, promising that she would see them soon.

She bravely waved goodbye and blew kisses. It was the last time Naismith saw his beloved mother. She was the only one who understood him. She encouraged his adventures, ideas, and inventions. She would listen to him as she baked or sewed. She laughed at his jokes and appreciated his gifts when he picked wildflowers for her or made her a project.

She contracted typhoid fever from her husband and died on November 6, 1870, on Naismith's ninth birthday and Annie's thirteenth. Their father had died a few weeks before, on October 19. Both were 37 years old and were buried quickly, with little fanfare, near the river island.

His grandmother Young and bachelor uncle Peter gave the children a home and lovingly did the best they could, but life never was the same for Naismith. Annie just got bossier. Naismith did what he could to help with Robbie and stay out of trouble. He spent most of his time in school, helping Uncle Peter with farm chores and playing with his friends at Bennies Corners.

He wasn't that enthusiastic about school, but he did enjoy the farm work. He especially liked playing with his friends. Grandma Young and Uncle Peter's house was halfway between Bennies Corners and Almonte. Every day after school and chores, Jim would meet his friends in front of the blacksmith shop in Bennies Corners. The boys invented games and contests. They would see who could lift the anvil the highest or swing the longest among the maple sugar bush trees behind the blacksmith shop. But by far, Naismith's favorite game was duck-on-a-rock.

It combined tag, marksmanship, alertness, good timing, and dodging ability. Naismith was fast and had great aim. In the game, a stone (the duck) is placed on a larger rock. One player guards the duck. The other players throw a stone, one at a time from about twenty feet, to try to knock the duck off the rock. If he's successful, he goes to the end of the line and waits for his next turn. The secret was in throwing the stone with right the arc. If a player missed, then the guard could chase him down and tag him, and then the tagged player would have to be the dreaded guard.

As a teen, Naismith often missed school due to farm chores. Soon he announced that he was stopping his education to devote himself to the farm, and in winter, he would work at the lumber camps. This met with disapproval from Annie because she knew about what went on at the camps.

The workers would tell dirty stories, pass a bottle around and many men took drinks. Naismith just smoked. He never took a drink because he knew his mother wouldn't approve. Besides, he had taken an oath with his brother Robbie that in the name of their mother they wouldn't drink. Of course, this oath was tested.

Once, Naismith was driving a sled and his path was blocked by men determined to bring him down and make him take a drink. He grabbed a sleigh stake and told the men that he would brain them if they didn't go on about their business. They made some advances but ultimately left Naismith alone. Those teen challenges helped him measure up to the kind of man his mother would want him to be.

★　★　★

Now he faced the dilemma of keeping his job. He had never been fired and he wasn't going to start that bad habit now. "Dear God," he prayed. "I just want to do something that will make the world a better place and help people grow. Right now, I must keep my job. If you see fit, please help me come up with a worthy game. Amen."

With that, Naismith opens the curtain and walks to the blackboard and erases all his previous ideas. He writes "Permanent Objective" as he repeats to himself, "Permanent Objective." Then he draws a line with a question mark at the end and a vertical line down the middle of the blackboard.

He mumbles, "Ball: Large. Small." On the left he writes "Large". On the right he scribbles "Small". Mahan knocks. Naismith quickly opens the door.

Jovially, Naismith says, "Come in! I have an idea for a game I'd like to run by you."

"Of course," Mahan replies.

"Remember when we practiced soccer in the gym and the playing space wasn't big enough?"

"Yes, I do. We had three bloody noses and a sprained thumb from that experiment."

Naismith continues, "But what was good about that experiment was the large ball."

Naismith goes to the blackboard and marks a circle around "Large" and asks, "Most Popular Game Today?"

Mahan answers, "Football is the most popular game." Then he adds, "Why can't this be used indoors?"

He grabs a pencil from Naismith's desk. Now the two men are jotting ideas and diagrams on paper.

"Tackling," Naismith admits as he paces in the room. "But why is tackling necessary?"

He leans back in his chair and props his feet upon the crowded desk.

"Because men are allowed to run with the ball," he says as he jumps from his seat. "If we can't run with the ball, we don't have to tackle; and if we don't tackle, …" He begins to scribble on his paper.

Mahan interrupts, mentioning, "Roughness will be eliminated."

Naismith hits his fist on the desk. "I've got it!" he exclaims. "A player has to throw the ball or bat it with his hand." He demonstrates by pretending to pass a ball to Mahan.

Naismith says, "Suppose a player runs, and a teammate throws the ball to him, and he has to stop or pass the ball immediately."

Mahan pretends to catch the ball. Quickly, Naismith hurries to his desk and writes, talking to himself.

"So far, we have a game that is played with a large, light ball; the players cannot run with the ball but must pass it or bat it with the hands; and the pass can be made in any direction."

Naismith leans back in his chair and folds his arms. Then Mahan, unconsciously leans back in his chair and folds his arms exactly like Naismith.

Naismith continues, "Now we need an objective for the players: a goal, like soccer, at each end of the floor." Naismith thinks aloud, "Accuracy is better than force. Throw the ball in an arc, and force has no value. So, pushing, tripping, and holding are fouls," he declares. Then he adds, "And a player would be disqualified if he did it again."

Naismith jigs around the office then exclaims, "Tossing up the ball between two teams is the fairest way of starting a game."

Mahan says, "One player from each team. Little chance for roughness."

Naismith points to the paper and says, "By golly, here's the fundamentals of a new game. We thank you, Lord. This will work! I just know it!"

Mahan glances at his watch. As he leaves, he adds enthusiastically, "I think so too! I look forward to trying it out with the team." Naismith jauntily pulls out a fresh scratch pad and quickly writes the "Thirteen Rules of A New Game." Soon Naismith hurries down the hall to the office of his secretary, Miss Lyons.

Miss Lyons is extremely skilled and her office is extremely neat. Just the opposite of Naismith's office. However, Miss Lyons forgives him. Naismith's appearance is always presentable and he's in excellent shape.

Miss Lyons, on the other hand, is plumpish and wears the same pink pilled "office sweater" every day. Her special gray "workers' smock" hangs on the coat rack, and she wears it for every assignment. She loves to type and has been caught doing it just for fun.

Her father was a Smith-Corona typewriter salesman/repairman, and she has every tool available for a typewriter. She keeps the tools cleaned and wrapped in a red towel, red being her dad's favorite color. Regularly, she loosens and oils her keys, a task few secretaries bother to do. That's the secret to her fast typing!

Baking is her hobby and she always has some kind of luscious goodie enclosed in a glass container for everyone in the office to munch on. Her friends have suggested that she enter her pecan pound cake into the Massachusetts State Fair but she never has. She feels her baking is God's work, and she doesn't need recognition for that.

When Naismith rushes in and drops off the Thirteen Rules, she's ready for the task.

"Miss Lyons, I'd be ever so grateful if you would type these rules for me and tack them to the gym bulletin board before the 11:30 practice Monday," Naismith requests.

"Yes, sir," Miss Lyons responds between a swallow of chocolate chip cookie and a sip of coffee.

She offers him a cookie, but Naismith waves her off with a gentle smile as he leaves. The minute he closes the door, she swallows the rest of her cookie, takes off her sweater, and dons her workers' smock. She assumes her position at the typewriter, takes a deep breath, and with military precision, quickly types the rules.

13 RULES OF BASKETBALL

1. The ball may be thrown in any direction with one or both hands.
2. The ball may be batted in any direction with one or both hands (never with a fist).

3. A player cannot run with the ball. The player must throw it from the spot from which he catches it, allowance to be made for a man who catches the ball when running at a good speed if he tries to stop.

4. The ball must be held in or between the hands; the arms or body must not be used for holding it.

5. No shouldering, holding, pushing, tripping or striking in any way the person of an opponent will be allowed; the first infringement of this rule by any player shall count as a foul, the second shall disqualify him until the next goal is made, or, if there was evident intent to injure the person, for the whole of the game, no substitute allowed.

6. A foul is striking at the ball with the fist, violation of Rules 3, 4, and such as described in Rule 5.

7. If either side makes three consecutive fouls, it shall count as a goal for the opponents (*consecutive* means without the opponents in the mean time making a foul).

8. A goal shall be made when the ball is thrown or batted from the grounds into the basket and stays there, providing those defending the goal do not touch or disturb the goal. If the ball rests on the edges, and the opponent moves the basket, it shall count as a goal.

9. When the ball goes out of bounds, it shall be thrown into the field of play by the person first touching it. In case of a dispute, the umpire shall throw it straight into the field. The thrower-in is allowed five seconds; if he holds it longer, it shall go to the opponent. If any side persists in delaying the game, the umpire shall call a foul on that side.

10. The umpire shall be judge of the men and shall note the fouls and notify the referee when three consecutive fouls have been made. He shall have power to disqualify men according to Rule 5.

11. The referee shall be judge of the ball and shall decide when the ball is in play, in bounds, to which side it belongs, and

shall keep the time. He shall decide when a goal has been made and keep account of the goals with any other duties that are usually performed by a referee.

12. The time shall be two 15-minute halves, with five minutes' rest between.

13. The side making the most goals in that time shall be declared the winner. In case of a draw, the game may, by agreement of the captains, be continued until another goal is made.

At exactly 11:30 a.m. on December 21, 1891, the Incorrigibles wander into the gym. Standing by the Thirteen Rules at the bulletin board, Naismith eyes the soccer balls stored against the wall. He picks one up and twirls it.

He utters, "Gentlemen, these are the Thirteen Rules of a new game. Please study them. Divide up nine to a team, three forwards, three backs and three centers. Let's try it."

Chase teases, "Not another new game!" Laughing, he throws off his sweatshirt and starts a round of jumping jacks. The others start to stretch and some do calisthenics.

Naismith tosses the ball to Mahan and replies, "I feel sure this is the one. If this game is a failure, I won't put you through any more experiments."

He blows his whistle and the men, seeing that Naismith means business, hover at the bulletin board.

Meanwhile, Pop Stebbins, the janitor who can fix anything, spots a rumpled edge of the gym floor. This is his favorite room to repair. Being a wrestler in his youth, he loves to be around the gym, even if it's as a custodian. He considers his job a blessing and is forever grateful.

Mr. Stebbins opens his toolbox, then he gets down on his knees and puts the side of his face parallel to the floor to see the problem. Ah! There it is: a warped board from the burst water pipe last year. It will have to be replaced, sanded, and stained the perfect color so it matches the rest of the floor. He rearranges old barrels and used baskets to make room for the floor repairs.

Naismith approaches him and asks, "Mr. Stebbins, do you have two boxes about eighteen inches square?"

Mr. Stebbins thinks for a moment then says, "No, I haven't any boxes, but I have those two old peach baskets in the corner, if they will do you any good."

Naismith looks and replies, "They will be just fine."

Then Naismith grabs a basket and takes a hammer and two nails from the toolbox. He springs up the stairs and attaches the basket to the railing which happens to be ten feet above the floor.

"Mr. Stebbins, please go nail the other basket at the opposite end just like this," Naismith requests.

Quickly, Mr. Stebbins attaches a basket to the other side. Naismith and two teams of nine head to center court. Each squad has the three forwards, three centers and three backs.

In what seems like slow motion, Naismith tosses up the first ball. All six centers leap for the toss-up and roughly battle each other for the ball. There's so much tackling, kicking, punching, and pushing that you would think this was a rugby free-for-all in the middle of the gym floor.

The players bumble around, often referring to the rules, and aggressively push and shove each other throughout the game. Fouls, black eyes, a dislocated shoulder, and a knockout put half the players on the bench.

Mr. Stebbins watches the men sort out this new running and flying-through-the-air game. He finds himself applauding when future teacher William Chase makes the first basket from twenty-five feet away. Everyone in the gym cheers, especially Naismith.

Buried in paperwork in his office next door, Gulick, the boss, overhears the commotion. Alarmed, he speedily stops in the gym and catches the sweaty men, excited with enthusiasm for this new game. Thinking he's seeing a miracle, he searches for Naismith and gives the relieved man a thumbs-up.

CHAPTER 3

MORE ABOUT MAUDE

Word has spread about the new game. Maude and other lady teachers from the local school drop by during lunch to check out the fun. The guys take full advantage. Chase receives the ball, he poises with it over his head to make a goal. When he's ready to throw, Mahan reaches up from behind and takes the ball out of his hands.

Chase pretends to wonder "Who did that?"

Then he proceeds to take the ball out of Mahan's hands when he tries the same shot. Mahan acts as if this is a surprise and tries the same antic again. The teachers laugh and applaud at all the funny business.

However, Maude has her mind on something else besides the new game. She spots Naismith on the sidelines. He catches her glance and shyly does a double take. Maude moves toward him.

She asks, "Is there any reason why women can't play this game?"

"I see no reason—"

Maude interrupts, "Good. I shall organize the first ladies' team."

Naismith stands in awe of her idea. He hadn't even thought of a ladies' team. "Please let me know if I can be of any assistance," he offers.

Maude gives him a lingering look and says, "I'm sure you can be."

She grabs a soccer ball from the sideline, then seductively walks off carrying the ball. Naismith is stunned with delight as he watches her tell the other ladies about her plan.

Suddenly, a class bell rings and Naismith jogs toward the bulletin board to get his rules. They're gone. He looks around but no one is there. A sad and bewildered Naismith heads toward his office.

Mahan blocks his path and asks, "You remember the rules that were put on the bulletin board?"

"Yes, I do," Naismith replies.

"They disappeared," Mahan says.

"I know it."

"Well, I took them. I knew this game would be a success and I took them as a souvenir. But I think now, you should have them." Mahan sheepishly hands the rules to Naismith.

"Thank you, Mahan. For me, a prized possession. I will enjoy watching how these 13 rules develop."

Patton and Chase stop next to Mahan on the way to the locker room. Other teammates continue playing in the background.

Mahan inquires, "What are you going to call the game? It can't just be called 'A New Game.'"

"I haven't thought about it. I've only been interested in getting it started."

"How about Naismith ball?"

Naismith laughs and says, "That name would kill any game."

They think a second, then together Mahan and Naismith say, "How about basket ball?"

"We have a basket and a ball. It seems to me to be a good name," Naismith decides.

"That's it! Basket ball!" the men agree. They give a cheer and head for the showers. A rogue ball spins past. Naismith is off and running to catch it.

A few days later, Maude is flirtatious and fun as she and several other ladies seriously attempt to play basketball in mutton sleeves and long skirts with bustles. It's a disaster! But the Incorrigibles cheer them on, and Naismith can't keep his eyes off Maude. When she attempts to make a basket and the ball bounces to the side, he captures the ball to help her.

He rushes up to her and says, "It's the right idea, but you need different clothes to move freely."

"We could just wear our bloomers."

"But then, the men couldn't watch," Naismith reveals.

"You like watching?"

Naismith smiles and stands beside her in shooting position.

"Let me show you how to shoot," he adds seriously.

Maude moves nearer and positions herself for the shot. Naismith can't breathe because Maude is so close to him. But being a professional, he does his best to analyze her natural skill.

As she reaches for the ball, their hands accidentally brush against each other. The world halts as they stop and gaze at each other. He quickly recovers and turns her around. Standing behind her, he guides her in making an overhead shot at the basket … and the ball goes in. They cheer as they try not to stare at each other. Naismith breaks away and retrieves the ball. They prepare to shoot again.

"Now, try it from your chest," Naismith says.

Maude carefully places her hands on the ball and Naismith stands behind her again. This time he tries to avoid touching her bosom. They shoot. Again, the ball goes in the basket. Maude turns toward him.

"Now what do I do?" Maude asks excitedly. Naismith seizes the moment and inquires, "The "Y" is having its annual Christmas party this Saturday. Will you join me?"

"Will you dance with me?"

"Yes, I will," he flirts.

"Then, I would be most delighted," she answers flirting back at him.

The "Y" decoration committee has outdone itself. The social room is beautiful, full of sumptuous garlands and a huge Christmas tree adorned with gold and silver ornaments. The scent of pine within the candle-lit room makes for a fairy tale evening.

Decked out in tuxedos, the best band in Springfield plays hits of the day and holiday favorites. Men look unusually handsome, and ladies chat easily in their most lavish party attire.

Maude stands to the side looking lovely as she sips her punch. She watches with pride when people surround Naismith. He tears himself away to be with her.

"Sorry, folks seem to have a lot of questions about basketball," he says.

"You're a champion and people love to be around champions," she gushes.

Suddenly, fast giddy music begins and Naismith grabs her hand.

"My dancing will change all that," he teases.

Crazy dancer Naismith turns Maude every way but loose. They're having the time of their lives showing each other steps they know, imitating each other, and just being together. When a slow song begins, they blend into each other's arms, aching to be as close as possible.

Slowly, they start to kiss and another couple bumps them. They continue dancing and start to kiss again, then the music switches to a fast beat. The people around them kick up their heels, but Naismith and Maude are still dancing slowly. Naismith takes charge and maneuvers Maude onto the balcony. As the snow gently falls, they look into each other's eyes and finally share their much-anticipated first kiss.

The next ten years fly by, spurred on by the fast spread of basketball throughout the Y.M.C.A. The Young Men's Christian Association was started in London on June 6, 1844, by George Williams and eleven friends. It was to be a safe refuge of Bible study and prayer for young men who had come to the city from rural areas and didn't want to get caught up in the temptations of a big city. It crossed English social classes and was to be a home away from home for students, sailors, and merchants. The idea spread rapidly across Europe, and in 1851, an American chapter was founded in Boston by Thomas Valentine Sullivan, a marine missionary.

By 1892, the 13 Rules were printed in wallet size, and it was not uncommon for every young boy to have a copy in his wallet. Basketball terms had become part of everyday vernacular, and college rivalries began, leading to some of the biggest rivalries today!

In June of 1894, Naismith and Maude married in Springfield. They sailed down the Connecticut River and on to Nova Scotia in bliss. The only fly in the soup was Maude's mother's embarrassment that her daughter had married a Northerner, a Yankee, a redcoat! Maude reminded her mother that the Civil War was over and that she would marry whomever she pleased.

They had their first child, Margaret, in 1895 in Springfield. They moved to Denver so that Naismith could pursue his interest in chiropractic medicine and so he could be the director of the Central Branch "Y" in that city. Maude was not happy about leaving her friends, family, and lifestyle. But she did her best to start a new life in Denver.

1897 was the scariest time in Naismith's life. When their second child, Hellen, was born, Maude came down with the dreaded typhoid fever. Since Naismith's parents had died of the disease, Maude's illness hit every fear button in his body. As a medical student and director of the "Y", he was gone a lot from home. He changed all that and cut down the hours as much as he could. He hired a nurse for Maude and took care of infant Hellen himself. He walked her in the night and took care of her feedings so Maude could rest. Fortunately, Maude recovered from typhoid, but unfortunately, it left her permanently deaf.

The vivacious, sharp-witted Maude had to learn to communicate by reading lips and signing. She handled it like a pro and immediately went to school to learn American Sign Language (A.S.L.). It was adapted from French Sign Language and brought to Hartford, Connecticut, in 1817 by Yale graduate and divinity student Thomas Hopkins Gallaudet. One of the first schools was the Kansas School for the Deaf, founded in 1866.

In 1898, Naismith joyfully graduated from Denver's Gross Medical College with a degree in chiropractic medicine. He got an athletic director job offer from the University of Kansas and promptly accepted. The university was located in Lawrence and the school for the deaf was nearby in Olathe. It was the perfect opportunity for him and his family.

They settled in and Jack was born in 1900. Maude Ann arrived in 1904. All this time, there was a constant frenzy over top basketball players and rival games. Women and kids played basketball with flair. The 13 Rules were expanded, improved, and streamlined with much debate, and Naismith was always in the middle of the fray. Life was busy, happy, and fulfilled, but change was inevitable.

CHAPTER 4

"QUIG" QUIGLEY
AND "PHOG" ALLEN

In 1905, Lawrence, Kansas, has paved streets and a progressive vibe. Autos and horses with buggies mix easily with each other. A source of pride is the University of Kansas. It has one of the most progressive sports programs west of the Mississippi. Clearly, this is the home of the Jayhawkers. To prove this, there are crimson and blue signs on billboards everywhere.

Dr. James Naismith, now 43, has his own chiropractic table in the corner of his office and two framed degrees above his desk, Doctor of Theology and Doctor of Chiropractic Medicine. This is the only tidy part. The rest of the office is an array of Cramer Brothers ointments, creams and liniments, skeletal frames, a Bible on top of a stack of papers, shelves full of books, and overstuffed filing cabinets.

Today, Naismith holds his baby, Maude Ann, and completes an interview with a new associate, Ernie "Quig" Quigley.

"My wife will be here shortly to pick up 'Exhibit A,'" Naismith informs Quig.

With pride, he holds up the diapered baby, who is marked with red and blue lines delineating muscle groups and tendons.

Naismith continues, "Here, at the Kansas University Athletic Department, all must work hard, have a physical, and learn to swim."

"I never heard of that, but sure. I just want to referee," Quigley responds.

"It's part of the new sports medicine program. You should do well here."

Suddenly there is a commotion outside the door. Maude, now in her late 30s and even more beautiful, escorts their five-year-old son, Jack, while she noisily pushes a baby carriage through the door. Jack breaks free and runs to his dad, who quickly swaddles the baby in his arms.

Naismith kisses Maude on the cheek.

"Maude," he says with a smile. Then he turns to Jack and gives him a big hug and says, "Hey, Buckeroo!" Maude abruptly sees Quigley.

"I'm sorry. I didn't see anyone," Maude says as she takes the baby. Naismith turns to his son and says, "I understand you have a sore tooth."

Naismith pulls out his wallet and gives Maude five dollars.

"For the dentist," Naismith adds.

"Thanks," Maude says. Then she signs, "I embarrassed you."

Naismith faces her directly so she can read his lips and lovingly says, "You most certainly did not."

Naismith speaks to Quigley yet faces Maude. Naismith says, "She had typhoid fever during her second pregnancy and has been deaf ever since."

Maude turns to Quig and says, "I read lips and we have our own signs. I talk and plenty. I just can't hear you!"

Jack holds his jaw and blurts, "It hurts, Father."

"We'll get it all fixed up," Naismith answers.

The baby's blanket falls to the side, revealing all the markings of 'Exhibit A'. Maude points to the baby and teases in Naismith's Scottish brogue, "Speaking of fixing, what is this?"

"Exhibit "A"," Naismith answers.

"Are you marking my baby?"

"I was merely demonstrating muscles and tendons."

"Oh, merely! Well, Dr. Naismith, you'll not be using any more of my babies for your merely demonstrating."

"Yes, Dearie," Naismith teases.

Their eyes twinkle as he gives her a little hug. Quigley tries not to laugh. She walks out the door coquettishly.

"Marriage. A grand institution," Naismith remarks.

Quigley and Naismith shake hands and Naismith walks him to the door. Quigley heads toward his physical and Naismith stops to see his secretary, Babs.

"Who's next?" Naismith asks as he takes his reading glasses from his breast pocket and puts them around his ears.

She checks her list as Naismith looks on and replies, "Phog Allen."

He smiles and says, "The hot-tempered star with the deep foghorn voice. Send him in."

Naismith returns to his desk, straightens his glasses, and twists the ends of his mustache.

★　★　★

Flashy dresser, Forrest "Phog" Allen is a strapping, physical specimen in his early 20s. He barges through the door with the charge of a bull. However, his outfit precedes him. He wears a suit of the brightest and flashiest plaid of the day, complete with a hat and a cane-style umbrella.

He shakes Naismith's hand eagerly and says, "Dr. Naismith, I couldn't get here fast enough. I understand there's a job for me?" Naismith takes one look at the outfit, collects himself by buttoning his gray flannel jacket, and has a seat behind his desk.

Naismith asks, "How's the back?"

"My playing days are over. Even my shooting won't save me."

"One of my favorite sights: you, standing about thirty-five feet from the basket, calmly dribbling the ball. Then you would turn abruptly and flick the darn thing in," quips Naismith.

"It's just a matter of timing and using the fingers. Now, I want to coach."

Naismith laughs and says, "You don't coach basketball! But—"

"Every other sport has a coach. Why not basketball? You act like someone who plants a grain of corn and thinks the seed simply grows," Phog bellows.

"Phog, it's a pastime, but, I've—"

Phog interrupts, "No, like a seed, it can be cultivated, fertilized, and watered."

Naismith files papers, opens the window, and turns on his fan as he listens.

Phog continues, "Basketball needs to be more entertaining and coaching will help that. Mostly at the college level. We can make a lot of money."

"Who needs a lot of money."

"Me. I need a lot of money," Phog answers.

"Basketball is for leisure; it's not designed to be boxing."

"But it can be. Look what happened to the Y.M.C.A. after only one year."

"That was the 'Y', not college," Naismith argues.

"That was madness! The Y.M.C.A. had to turn away a thousand-plus memberships because men and even women wanted to play basketball."

"It's not business! It's education," Naismith answers heatedly.

"It is business! Even now, we need a bigger college competition," Phog suggests.

"Yes, we do. Call it something simple: The U.S. College Challenge."

"No," Phog demands. "Something more exciting and exhilarating! Like 'Winner Take All' or 'March Madness'."

"You and your ideas. You're taking this too far."

Quigley walks by and overhears the heated conversation. Naismith spots him and is relieved for a break from Phog's diatribe. "Mr. Quigley, meet Phog Allen," Naismith says.

Quigley extends his hand and says admiringly, "Oh, Coach Allen. You're legendary. I saw you win the Duke game."

Phog beams and replies, "Thank you. Thank you for your support."

"Quigley here says he wants to referee."

Quigley swiftly intervenes. "Yep. Baseball. Basketball. I want to go all the way to the Olympics!"

Naismith and Phog exchange a look as Quigley leaves for his next class.

Phog jumps back into the conversation, saying, "Yes! Basketball in the Olympics."

"Another idea! You're exhausting me!" Naismith complains.

Phog won't let this opportunity go and blurts, "It's an international sport now. All it takes is a nomination and an acceptance. I'll start a letterwriting campaign to the International Olympic Committee today!"

Exasperated, Naismith hands him a note and says, "First do this. Here's the person to call for a basketball coaching position at Baker University. It's up the road and they asked for you."

"Really! Thank you, Dr. Naismith, thank you!" He shakes Naismith's hand and rushes out.

As Naismith sits, he can't help wondering about Phog's idea. He twirls his mustache again and stares out the window.

He says out loud, "Who would even want to go to the Olympics?"

CHAPTER 5

JOE FORTENBERRY

It's 1929 and we're in Happy, Texas. Over the past twenty years, basketball has grown tremendously. The rules are more specific and the teams are made up of five players, not nine, such as on the original team. Now it's normal to have football in the fall, basketball in the winter, and baseball in the spring and summer, even in small towns.

★   ★   ★

At 17, blonde hair and blue-eyed Joe Fortenberry is a gangly 6'8". He's handsome and clever but is completely oblivious to who he is or what he looks like. All he knows is that he loves basketball and his pants are always too short.

After several crop failures and their house burning to the ground, his family moved from the small North Texas town of Joy to Happy, a community in the Texas panhandle, with cheap, flat farmland. No one wanted to leave all the aunts, uncles, and cousins in the Fortenberry clan, especially Joe. He had people coming to look at his basketball talents for college scholarships, and what if they couldn't find him!

Now, he dribbles in the rain and practices long shots, aiming the ball at his basketball goal on the side of the barn. His dad, Oliver, a worn farmer of 45, rocks in a dilapidated chair on his front porch and reads in his newspaper about the "Crash". Callie, Joe's hardworking mother, serves dinner to his two brothers and four sisters.

"Oliver, please call Joe. His dinner is getting cold," she calls.

"He'll be there directly, Callie."

Callie comes out the door, dish towel in hand, ready to give Oliver a piece of her mind.

She notices Oliver calmly rocking with the paper in his hands and asks, "What are you reading about?"

"The Crash and how they're trying to get basketball into the Olympics."

Callie exclaims, "What?"

"Here's the full article by Phog Allen, *The International Growth of Basketball*. It says over 18,000,000 people play the game." Callie sighs and Oliver motions for her to look at Joe dribbling in the rain.

Callie says, "I never saw anybody so sad and lonely. He'll be slow to make friends. Moving him from Joy to Happy in his senior year … meanest thing we've ever done."

"Not to worry, Mother. When they see him play basketball, he'll have plenty of friends."

★ ★ ★

With the Great Depression in full swing, Joe did everything he could to make money for the family. They depended on him and he didn't want to disappoint anyone.

One evening in 1932, Model T Fords are circled in a dried-out creek basin with their blaring front headlights facing the center. A welterweight boxing match is under way. Men bet wildly. Bawdy women cheer them on. Mickey, a young, arrogant boxer ambles toward Jeb, the local ringmaster.

Mickey asks, "Where's this Joe Fortenberry guy? He's got five minutes, then I leave."

Jeb just doesn't have the patience for Mickey and tries to get away from him.

"Hush up, Mickey. He'll be here. He promised the town council."

"I'm ready for the money. I need some new diamonds," Mickey brags.

"It's the Depression and you're talkin' about diamonds. Joe's splittin' his win with the city."

"He ain't gonna' win. So, course, he's sayin' that."

Jeb winces at Mickey's self-centeredness, yet holds his temper and chides, "We'll see." The crowd cheers as the welterweights finish. Jeb hurries away to help distribute the bets. A boy tears away from the crowd and stands on a car hood viewing the field. Two headlights come up the road. The boy yells excitedly, "He's here! Joe's here!"

Men jump into their cars and make a path for Joe's Model T. It's like a parting of the waters, there is so much reverence for Joe. He's become a reserved man who doesn't say much. He does his talking with sports, especially on the basketball court. Wearing a letter jacket, he smoothly drives into the middle of the circle. Mickey has his gloves on and is pent up and ready to win. He leans toward Joe's window, takes a swing at Joe, and misses.

Mickey says, "Hey, Jerk, get out and fight."

Joe doesn't even bother to get out of the car. He quickly extends his long arm with its huge mittlike fist and knocks Mickey out cold. The crowd is stunned. Joe simply turns the car around and drives off as the crowd comes to life with whoops and hollers.

Meanwhile, the Fortenberrys load into the family auto to go see Joe play in the West Texas State Teachers College basketball game. Even with dyslexia, Joe got a full basketball scholarship, and the family is very proud of him. Game night is the highlight of the week. They wear the team colors, maroon and white, and carry folded banners.

At the gym, it's a full house of fans and lots of pretty girls. There's no problem spotting the Fortenberrys. They're the big, tall family at center court with the banners that say "Go Joe" and "Go Buffaloes".

As the rival teams warm up, Joe quickly changes into his uniform and ties his size 14 shoes. Earl, a trainer, hands an envelope to Joe.

Earl says, "Here's your half from the fight."

Joe nods and says, "Thanks. Just give it to my mother. Tell her it's for groceries."

He hurries to the court to join the team, and the crowd cheers when they see him. When Joe sees Earl give Callie the envelope, he waves to her and his mother blows him a kiss.

During the warm-up before the game, the crowd chants "Joe, Joe, Joe" when he jumps high and, with his hand above the rim of the basket, shoots downward, dunking the ball. Coach Sam Burton, a conservative middle-aged man catches Joe dunking and goes ballistic!

Burton blows his whistle, rushes onto the court, and yells, "Fortenberry, you're on the bench! I told you, no high lay-ups!"

"You said in the game! This is before the game."

"Are you mocking me? Are you trying to ruin basketball? That shot is too flashy, ungentlemanly, and undignified for the game."

Livid, Coach Burton sends Joe to the bench. The crowd boos.

CHAPTER 6

PHOG AND THE 1932 OLYMPICS

In 1932, Phog Allen's Kansas University office is full of Jayhawker memorabilia, products with Phog's picture plastered on them, and many awards. Phog, now 44 years old, fills a small suitcase with books. Naismith, now a spry 68, drops by.

Naismith asks, "Packing up for Los Angeles?"

"Just some reading material. I decided to take Bessie and the kids with me to see the Olympics."

"Pretty expensive," Naismith comments.

Phog stops packing and stares at Naismith, and the never-ending argument starts again.

"You could go, too! If you would just accept money for endorsements."

Insulted, Naismith replies, "Basketball is my gift to the world."

"Your 'gift' is making me rich. It could make you rich as well."

"Your picture is all over basketballs and ointments! It's cheap and tacky."

Phog rolls his eyes and patiently adds, "My wife doesn't count every penny like Maude. If you won't do it for yourself, do it for her."

"I'm doing what I think is right."

Phog patiently says, "You've given so much. What is right, is for you to let yourself receive. You're really bad at that. People want to do things for you, honor you, and you always rebuff them. It hurts their feelings. You're supposed to receive as well, you know."

Naismith says, "It's more blessed to give than to receive. Acts 20:35."

Realizing that the argument is futile, Phog quips, "Whoever sows bountifully will also reap bountifully. Corinthians 9:6! You have sown bountifully. Yet, my family will frolic on the beach and see the Games."

"And you'll mingle with the International Olympic Committee," Naismith adds, relieved that Phog is changing the subject.

"You know me well," he replies. "So far, they have been very open to basketball. Since Germany is the 1936 host country, they decide if basketball gets to be a full event."

"Tell Avery Brundage I said 'Hello.'"

Phog blurts, "I'll shake all the necessary hands. I think we can do it. The sport is just too international now. It would make Germany look bad to say "no," and Germany doesn't want to look bad to the millions of people around the world that play basketball."

The next day, Phog, his fashionable wife and three happy kids land at the United Airport in sunny California. As the palm trees sway, Phog settles his family, then goes to every social event and meeting that the 1932 Olympics has to offer.

Back in Lawrence, Naismith and Maude sit at the kitchen table paying bills. They're short on the mortgage again and realize the consequences if they don't pay it. Naismith is distraught, but the ever-faithful Maude is optimistic that the money will come from somewhere.

Meanwhile, Phog shakes hands with the handsome and successful Avery Brundage. He's head of the International Olympic Committee and also the head of the American Olympic Committee. This closed-door meeting is Phog's most important. Only the host country can allow a new sport into their Olympics, but Avery Brundage is a master at helping people make a productive decision. If Brundage agrees, then there's a good chance basketball will be in the 1936 Berlin Olympics.

CHAPTER 7

GAS AND GOLD

In 1933, outside the Echo Café in McPherson, Kansas, a sign reads: Beware: Kansas Is a Dry State. Kansas had statewide prohibition from 1881 to 1948 and still has a strict and highly regulated approach to alcohol. As of April 2017, Kansas had not ratified the 21st Amendment, which ended nationwide prohibition in 1933, and there remain three dry counties.

The Echo Bar was in full use before 1881 as an establishment for the consumption of alcoholic beverages. In 1933, it's used as a local restaurant. Still, people come to the bar, sit on the antique stools and order lemonade or a Prohibition cocktail.

Behind the bar, there is a black chalkboard for sports scores. The radio blasts music and sports news. Telegraph runners from next door update the scoreboard as soon as possible. "McPherson Refiners" is front and center and in the largest letters. Abe, a kind man of mixed heritage, polishes glasses. I. A. O'shaughnessy strolls in for a libation.

Abe greets him, "Hello, sir. What can I get for the owner of Globe Oil? Maybe, a Prohibition Sour?"

I. A. is in no mood for frivolity. He's got a lot on his mind and is taking a much-needed breather from the office.

"No sissy drinks for me," he says. "I need a score check and a special coffee. Not necessarily in that order."

Abe serves the coffee and asks, "So how's it goin' at the refinery?"

Then Abe turns and adds homemade gin to a water glass with ice. I. A. takes a generous swig of the "water," then sips on the coffee and says, "It's going well. Now, I need more advertising for my gasoline."

"Sounds like a good problem to have."

"In a day, I have 200,000 gallons to sell and a lot of competition."

"You have those new gas stations," Abe mentions.

"Yep. But the ads for them are expensive. I need an edge. Something different and more fun."

I. A. stares at the chalk board pensively.

Abe says, "You have the basketball team."

"It's ready to go national."

Abe comments, "Big risk. Big gain."

I. A. takes another swig of his water then laments, "Big decision."

He takes a contemplative look at the printed McPherson Refiners on the chalkboard and adds, "That coach, Gene Johnson, up at Wichita State, he's won the American Athletic Union Championship three times in a row."

"Naismith/Phog Allen protégé," Abe acknowledges. "Yes, three-time A.A.U. champ. Now at Ogden. But he's here tonight coaching the exhibition game."

"I know. I'll be there." Then I. A. asks, "When people come in, what scores do they check first?"

Abe laughs and says, "It's February, so basketball, and with so many games coming up, let's just say, I sell a lot of coffee."

I. A. stands and stretches, then adds, "Abe, thanks for listening. You've helped a lot. In fact, on that scoreboard, get rid of "McPherson". Put "Globe" in front of "Refiners"."

Abe erases McPherson and boldly prints GLOBE, adding, "That looks good."

"Especially if we win," I. A. teases.

CHAPTER 8

THE OLYMPICS AND JOHN McLENDON

Meanwhile, in Naismith's office at Kansas University, Naismith shuffles papers and tries to get organized. It's agonizing. He hates filing. He soon gets relief when Phog rushes in wearing a tweed jacket, yellow tie, and red socks. He waves a letter, exclaiming, "We got it! We actually got in! We're in the Olympics. Basketball is in the Olympics!"

Naismith stops, grabs the letter to read, and exclaims, "I don't believe it! We have disagreed on many things. But you did it. Now, let us be able to lose gracefully and win courteously."

"No!" Phog demands. "We're gonna show the world!"

Naismith sighs, "We have more pressing issues right here in Kansas. You think too big." Phog doesn't hear a word Naismith is saying. He's already planning.

"We'll recruit the best team we can find, and America will win the first Olympic Gold Medal in basketball," Phog exclaims as he rushes out of Naismith's office.

On the way out, he accidentally slams the door and nearly runs over young John McLendon, a 5'8" skinny black kid carrying a basketball. John doesn't seem to mind. He's nervously looking for a room number and spots Naismith's name on a door. When he stands before it, he takes a breath and pulls out his lucky 50-cent piece, flips it, then knocks.

Naismith asks through the door, "Who is it?"

John answers, "I'm John McLendon Jr. from Kansas City. My major is physical education, and I understand that you're my advisor."

"Come in. Have a seat," Naismith says.

John shyly enters, rubbing his 50-cent piece between his thumb and index finger, and says, "My dad told me to find you. He said you would look after me because you're color blind."

"Well, fathers are always right," Naismith jokes. "Did he give you that 50-cent piece?"

"Yes, for good luck."

"What's your goal?"

John answers, "I've wanted to be a basketball coach since I watched a player shooting baskets as a young boy."

Naismith smiles wryly and says, "Through the years, I've found out that basketball coaching is quite an art. It takes more than just playing the game."

"And that's what I'm here to learn," John replies earnestly.

"To get your degree and be part of our new sports medicine program, you have to work hard, have a physical, and be proficient in swimming."

"I'll work hard, sir. I want this more than anything, and I'll take any job you can give me for extra money. I'm in tip-top shape. I was a lifeguard in Kansas City."

Naismith says, "Good! You should do well here."

CHAPTER 9

THE SWIMMING POOL AND KANSAS UNIVERSITY 1933

John climbs out of the outdoor pool and heads for the showers. He looks forward to a swim every morning. A workout with laps in each of the strokes sets his day and keeps him in shape. However, at this pool, onlookers stare and wonder. Black maintenance men stand by waiting for him to leave.

In the locker room, John showers and dresses. There are a few other blacks, but mostly whites. The blacks stick to themselves. The whites go on about their business.

Outside, John walks past the maintenance men draining the pool. He stops and asks, "Is this a routine draining? Or is this being done because I just finished swimming?"

The overworked maintenance leader says in a rather condescending manner, "Use your own judgment."

Disgusted, John says, "I hope Kansas University has a lot of money for water, because I'll be swimming every day." He walks off and the men begin to drain the pool. Heading toward his dorm, John spots "DO NOT SWIM WITH THE NEGRO" signs. He gathers them, sprints to Naismith's office and shows him the offensive words.

It took many years, but gradually, and with great discipline, Naismith had learned to control his temper. Now he had to use all his control to calmly reply, "From time to time, some people are prejudiced and ignorant, but don't let that stop you. Come with me and bring those signs. We're going to see the Chancellor."

On the way, Naismith and John walk by Phog Allen's office. John sees Phog's title on the door, "Head Basketball Coach" and smiles and says to himself, "Someday, I'll be a coach too."

Hastily, Naismith leans in Phog's doorway, interrupts his phone conversation, and says, "Phog, please accompany us."

Now, Phog has known Dr. Naismith for many years and has studied him closely. If Naismith says to come with him, that's exactly what he will do, especially when the tone of his voice is so serious. Phog quickly hangs up the phone and follows them. John's in heaven. He's walking with Naismith and Phog Allen, two of his heroes.

Naismith walks right past the secretary and into the Chancellor's office. The Chancellor, a man in his sixties, sees Naismith and immediately stops what he is doing and stands to greet him. Naismith motions to John for the signs. John quickly gives them to him. With great compassion, Naismith shows the Chancellor and Phog the signs. Both stare at them in disbelief.

Angrily, Naismith says, "Chancellor, my star athlete, and the person that I employ to drive for me and my wife, found these signs on our campus today."

The Chancellor puts on his glasses more for taking time to think than to read and says, "Horrifying." Then he says to John, "I'm so sorry. Even though Kansas is a free state and Negroes are welcome here, some people simply have not gotten the message."

Naismith responds, "Let me make this easy for you, Chancellor. I've been part of Kansas University Athletics for 35 years. If I ever see another sign like this, I'll resign and find another university!"

The Chancellor doesn't like being threatened, and he definitely does not want to lose Naismith. He replies, "I assure you that this will be resolved immediately!"

Phog pulls John to the side and says, "The only reason you can't go swimming is, as head of the Athletic Department, I am responsible for your safety." John gives his idol a long look. Safety has always been an issue for his race, and here Phog is, in typical Phog style, telling it like it is.

"I have a deal for you," John suggests.

"Okay."

John says, "Keep the pool open two weeks for everybody. If there's no incident, then open the pool for the colored."

Naismith immediately responds, "Agreed! The Chancellor nods and shouts, "Agreed!

Later that evening, John and other black students mingle at a dorm social hall with a sprinkling of whites headed by white friend and fellow athlete Jack Lovelace. He waves a paper and asks, "Is there anyone here who hasn't signed the petition?" One white student raises his hand. Lovelace goes to him.

John stands and addresses the group, saying, "Those of you who are one of the fifty black students enrolled at Kansas University, please don't go near the pool for the next two weeks."

Lovelace speaks up. "Our petition says that we do not object to swimming with colored students." The group applauds and Jack continues, "And there's already over a thousand signatures." The group whoops and applauds again.

"Thank you, Mr. Lovelace! If there are no incidents, they will open the pool for everybody."

Lovelace leans in to John and asks, "How can we fix that?"

John hooks an arm around his friend and says, "How can there be an incident if colored folks aren't there?" The group laughs and cheers. John says, "All who agree say 'Aye'."

The group responds with a loud and clear "Aye!"

Two weeks later, John watches as blacks and whites enjoy the pool. A couple of very large football players and Lovelace stand guard. There's not a hint of any kind of disturbance. Naismith and Phog stroll by to check the situation and they like what they see.

Naismith waves at John and he waves back. Then Phog boldly grabs John's arm and pulls him to the side and says, "You're clever John, a regular smart aleck. I hear you want to coach."

"Yes, sir. More than anything."

Naismith joins them and Phog continues, "Let Dr. Naismith advise you and then go to as many of my games as you can. You may have what it takes to be a pretty good coach."

Naismith shakes John's hand and says, "Remember, John, being a bit of a smart aleck is part of what it takes to coach basketball!" John smiles and understands that he just passed a test in Naismith's eyes. Naismith continues, "You had a problem and you solved it. This happens every second in a basketball game! Thinking fast on your feet is a prerequisite for a player and a coach."

"Yes, sir," John says as he accepts his praise wholeheartedly.

CHAPTER 10

COACH GENE JOHNSON

The American Athletic Union was founded January 1, 1888. Its mission was to promote amateur athletics for all ages. Kids could join and many remained as adults. After college and the Olympics, this organization was the last stop since there was no professional basketball at the time. The National Basketball Association (N.B.A.) was launched in 1949 to promote professional basketball with the highest ethics and standards. But in 1933, businesses would sponsor A.A.U. teams and players to advertise their products. A winning team meant a winning product. Rival signage was just as competitive as the game.

Now, at the McPherson gym, the Ogden/Refiners exhibition game is underway. There's the Hillyard Chemical "Chemists" We Invented the Floor Shine in Basketball sign. A Wichita Henry Clothiers "Henrys" streamer featuring a smiling Coach Gene Johnson and his team as models in sharp outfits adorning the wall. In large letters, the banner says Three Time A.A.U. Champs. Also, there's a GLOBE OIL—CLEAN AND CLEAR GASOLINE oversized pennant.

I. A. O'shaughnessy, Naismith, Phog, and John McLendon and are in the stands. This is a special night and the gym is packed. Peppy girls cheer. Quigley referees and the players concentrate on every move. The Henrys are ahead. Near the end of the game, Coach Gene Johnson, motions for a time-out. His new Ogden team huddles.

Gene blasts them, "Kansas is my home state and you're embarrassing me! Pass the ball down the court! Nobody wants to see your fancy dribbling; they want a score."

In an exciting finish, the Ogden team rallies to win 46-34. Gene Johnson is elated. When the disappointed Wichita Henrys fans leave, reporters chase Coach Johnson as he runs for the locker room. I. A. looks at the scoreboard, smiles to himself, then nods "yes" to Naismith and Phog.

Later, in the sweaty locker room, the team celebrates with club soda, spewing it everywhere and on each other. Just outside, John McLendon accompanies Naismith and Phog to congratulate the team. Gene greets them and makes a huge effort to shake Naismith's and Phog's hands. They are royalty to him. Naismith quickly introduces John, "And this is my newest star, John McLendon. He wants to be—"

John interrupts "... like you, Coach Johnson."

Gene shakes John's hand, "You're in the right place and we need to integrate. Many black athletes have a lot of talent. Do as Dr. Naismith and Phog say, and maybe you can win in college and the A.A.U."

"I will, sir. I will," John pledges.

As the team celebrates, I. A. steps into the locker room. Gene pretends he doesn't know I. A. is there and arrogantly makes I. A. walk up to him.

I. A. asks Gene, "Out on the town?"

"Of course. We won tonight."

I. A. continues, "I'm I. A. O'shaughnessy of the Globe Oil Refinery."

"I know who you are," Gene acknowledges. They shake hands briefly.

"I've decided that I want to go to the Olympics, and I need a coach that wants to win as much as I do."

Gene inquires, "I hear you have lots of gasoline to sell."

"And I hear you have the recruiting and coaching skills to win Olympic Gold." Gene nods, buttons his sports jacket, and says, "I choose the team."

"Of course," I. A. agrees.

"I need pay and all in writing, and I have to resign from Ogden. I'm committed to them for a year."

"You can recruit from there and have a team together for '35. Win the A.A.U. championship in '36 and then win gold at the Olympics," I. A. strategizes. Gene looks in his eyes, impressed with his plan.

"Clean and clear," Gene sums up.

"Clean and clear. Just like my gasoline," I. A. adds without blinking. Gene sees that he's dealing with a man who's direct and to the point.

"Just like your gasoline," Gene agrees. This time, they shake hands solidly.

Naismith joins them when he sees that the deal has been made and says, "Congratulations, gentlemen. I think this is a good match."

"We agree," they respond. "We agree."

The main way teams made money in 1934 was to barnstorm. They would travel throughout the country, play exhibition games, and split the box office after all expenses had been paid. The goal was to barnstorm as much as possible so a team could practice in real games, make money, and capitalize on the free advertising. Phog, Gene, and I. A. mapped out a plan to prepare for the Olympics.

One such event is in Mexico during a pouring rain. The enthusiastic Mexican team chases the American team all over the muddy court using a 2-on-1 strategy. At the half, Gene rushes to a phone booth and dials. After a few rings, Phog picks up the phone. Gene doesn't even give him a chance to say "Hello" and shouts angrily, "Phog, why in the hell am I here in blasted Mexico? In the rain, for God sakes."

Phog booms through the phone, "Because basketball is in the Olympics. I've worked all my career for this. We better look good internationally or our sport won't be included again. Put on a show."

Gene yells, "The Mexicans are outrunning us. It's like we're chasing loose pigs and the pigs are winning."

"You better get their playbook or we'll look like fools."

Gene replies, "Oh, I have it. There's one move I'm calling the fullcourt zone press."

"Get the hell out of there before we look worse," Phog advises.

"I'm going to Texas next. I got a tip on a 6′8″ center named Joe Fortenberry."

Pretty girls walk by the phone booth and distract him. "I'll get back to you," Gene says, as he hangs up the phone and to check out the girls.

★   ★   ★

But even Gene Johnson doesn't have much time for the ladies. Now he's at West Texas State Teachers College watching for Joe Fortenberry. Gene is in the stands catching the pre-game activities, scouting the players and the crowd. The West Texas team, nearly all around 5′10″, files out to dazzle the fans with various warm-up antics. When Joe lopes out, the crowd goes wild. Gene takes note. Joe leaps high for a tip-off and easily governs the ball. Gene knows right then and there that if he has Joe for his center, he can win gold at the Olympics.

CHAPTER 11

HITLER AND LENI, LAEMMLE AND FRANKENSTEIN

In 1935, Adolf Hitler, at age 45, is finally dictator. He's worked hard for his position. Germany had been in a recession for years and was still trying to convince the world of its innocence in regard to the World War 1 crimes of using poisonous gas and unnecessary brutality. The country had been banished from various trade agreements and banned from the Olympics in 1920 and 1924.

Hitler became leader of the year-old National Socialist German Workers' Party (Nazi) in 1921. He was mentored by far-right founder and politician Anton Drexler. The purpose of the party was to unify all German-speaking people and territories so a master race could be developed that would dominate the world. Jews, blacks, homosexuals, and people with any kind of disability had to be eliminated.

First, the territories must be consolidated. A coup to seize power was staged in 1923 at a popular beer hall in Munich, Bavaria. Two thousand Nazis, including Hitler, marched, but they were halted by the police. The plan failed and Hitler was wounded in the process. That year he went to jail for nine months for treason.

There he wrote *Mein Kampf* (*My Struggle*), his treatise on what Germany needed to do to become a world power. He also perfected his oration skills to move a crowd to frenzy, action and/or tears. When he got out of jail, he reorganized the Nazi Party and convinced the Germans that if he was Fuhrer, all would thrive. He envisioned a thousand years of light, dominance, and prosperity for all Germans, and the ruse worked!

His right-hand man, Joseph Goebbels, a frail and mousy megalomaniac, had a wife and six daughters. Yet, he was a lady chaser and power whore. He enjoyed his influence over Hitler and was very instrumental in his election. He was proud of his sly way of manipulating Hitler to see things his (that is, Goebbels') way.

As is the daily office routine, Goebbels hands Hitler a German newspaper. Then he adds an English newspaper. Then newspapers from other European countries, and last, *The New York Times*.

Goebbels mentions, "As your Propaganda Minister, I congratulate you, Fuhrer, on the worldwide box office success of *Triumph of the Will*."

This film was a documentary written, produced, and directed by Leni Riefenstahl. Goebbels hired Riefenstahl to make a movie glorifying Hitler and the Nazi party. Hitler was the executive producer and his name is in the opening credits. It was a huge success and helped Hitler see that film was an excellent propaganda tool.

"The reviews are quite good, I must say. Good work, Goebbels."

Hitler starts back to his desk, reading the reviews again.

Goebbels says, "I think we should commission Leni to make a movie about the Olympics."

Hitler turns up his nose, lets out a sigh, and says, "Riefenstahl? Olympics? We don't even need the Olympics. Why waste money on this?"

"The Olympics will show the world we aren't barbarians," Goebbels reminds Hitler. "People love movies, and people go to see heroes in movies. You will be the hero of *Olympiad*."

"And Leni can show that we are the superior people of the world," Hitler summarizes. Goebbels can't help but gloat. He knows he's a master of propaganda and manipulation, and he's proven it yet another time.

"Exactly, Fuhrer. An exhibition of the 1000 years of Supreme Rule you so eloquently speak of."

Hitler saunters to a window that faces the street and asks, "By the way, did they close the Jewish shops on the square?"

"Yes, that was done this morning," Goebbels explains.

"No Jews. No Negroes. They can't be seen in the movie. Aryans only."

"Of course, Fuhrer," Goebbels replies.

Meanwhile, in a Universal Pictures screening room, middle-aged Carl Laemmle, the sole owner of Universal Pictures, sits front row center in a comfy leather seat watching "dailies," film shot the day before. He's a German Jew who escaped with his family during the Russian Revolution. He discovered nickelodeons in Chicago, but instead of watching the shows, he watched the crowds that flocked to see the shows. He quickly surmised that this business was a money maker. If he moved to California, where the weather was sunny most days, he could make more movies. The logic was correct and now he was living a fruitful life in balmy Los Angeles, enjoying everything the "land of the free" had to offer.

Now, he smokes a cigarette and checks dailies of *The Bride of Frankenstein*, starring Boris Karloff. A light flashes on his side console. He presses a button and answers, "Yes, June."

"Jack Pierce is here about the Frankenstein neck bolts and the basketball team."

"Send him in," Laemmle says cheerfully.

Jack Pierce is in his forties and short and stocky. He's the top make-up artist at Universal Pictures, and he got there by merging sculpture and unusual make-up combinations. He has always thought of himself as more of a scientist than a make-up man and wears his customary white lab coat. He carries a Frankenstein head for his boss to approve. Laemmle greets him warmly.

"Jack, my favorite make-up artist!"

"Hi, Mr. Laemmle. We're right on track. We've cut the Frankenstein make-up procedure to seven hours."

"Very good," Laemmle says. But to Laemmle the make-up is a given. What excites him now is the basketball team. He became interested in sports when he helped Germany enter the Olympics in 1932 because the country was in a deep economic depression. Soon Laemmle found out that Pierce loved basketball and had formed a makeshift team on the Universal lot. When the team started winning, Laemmle saw the advertising opportunity and encouraged Pierce.

Laemmle asks, "How's the basketball team?"

"Sir, to go to the Olympics, we need a coach for the Universals."

Needing a pause, Laemmle puts out his cigarette slowly and gently says, "Jack, I know you've worked hard for our team and I appreciate that, but America isn't going to the Hitler Olympics. With the political climate like it is, I'm bringing in Jews every month."

"To your credit, sir," Pierce adds.

"The U.S.A. won't tolerate barbaric treatment of other human beings," Laemmle says, as he finishes putting out his cigarette.

Pierce interjects, "But most Americans don't believe the threat is real. They want the thrill of the Olympics."

"Supporting the Berlin Games is out, Jack. If the boys decide to go, their jobs aren't guaranteed when they come home. That's the amateur rule of the Olympic code.

"They know that, sir. But, they would like your blessing."

To change the mood, Laemmle lights another cigarette and says, "I love basketball; the Frankenstein bit at our games has the audience screaming. You're doing a great job. It's terrific publicity. The kind you can't buy."

"Thank you, sir," Pierce says.

"Here's what I'll do. I won't support the team if it goes to Berlin. As a Jew, I can't do that. But I want you to milk every dime of publicity around the Olympics. I don't want to be the guy who said "no" since it probably won't happen anyway. Kapiesch?"

Pierce nods then adds, "I'll use the money we have to do whatever is needed. Maybe an interim coach."

Several lights blink on the console.

"Are we done?" Laemmle asks.

Pierce shows him the Frankenstein head and says, "We lengthened the neck. Now you can see the electricity going through the bolts better."

Laemmle examines the Frankenstein head and says, "Yes, more exciting. We're on schedule to shoot Monday morning!" The light on the console blinks again. Laemmle steps to the console as Pierce starts to leave.

"The *Showboat* team is here," June says.

Laemmle speaks into the console, "I'll be right there." Then he turns to Pierce and says, "Gotta' run. Anything else?"

"No, sir. We'll do what we can about the Olympics, sir."

"Good man, Jack. Good man," Laemmle utters as he dashes out the door to his next meeting.

CHAPTER 12

JOE FORTENBERRY—
HOME AWAY FROM HOME

At 25, Joe has accomplished all he can in Happy. Now he's moving on to the next stage of his life, a high-paying job at the Globe Oil Refinery in McPherson, Kansas. He eagerly finishes loading his Model T and, with a tear in his eye, hugs each family member. Last, he hugs his parents and says, "I love you. Thank you for all you've done for me."

He turns and leaps into his car. Callie does her best not to cry and says to Oliver, "He's a good boy with a good job in an oil boomtown. He'll do fine."

Oliver comforts her to contain his own emotions and adds, "Who knew a little town like McPherson, Kansas, would be the heart of basketball. You're right, he'll be fine."

Joe drives off in a cloud of dust and travels through the flat, treeless countryside. The dirt gets less and less as he leaves the dustbowl. A few hours later, there's a Welcome to Kansas sign. Joe proceeds to McPherson and views numerous oil derricks, pumpjacks, and the glistening refinery.

★   ★   ★

At the Globe Refinery sports office, Joe ducks his head through the doorway and hurries to greet Coach Johnson. They shake hands warmly.

Gene says, "Joe, good to see you. Drive okay?"

"Fine, sir."

"We have your locker ready. Go suit up and then we'll meet the team."

"Yes, sir."

Inside the locker room, Joe gazes at the pristine sports mecca. It's the nicest locker room he's ever seen and he's impressed. A locker with his name already on it. A warm-up suit. Sweats and Converse shoes, size 14. Tom, a trainer, brings fresh towels.

"Hope these will do," Tom says, referring to the sweats. "Tomorrow you'll be fitted for your dress suits."

"The sweats are fine. A suit?"

"Yep! We're the best-dressed team on the circuit. Coach wants us to be courteous and dapper. We're the tallest, wildest, and nattiest."

"I've never had a real suit," Joe confides, but Tom has already left the room. Joe quickly changes and confidently trots to the court.

Joe can't miss dark-haired Willard Schmidt, about 25 years old, 6'9" and heavier built. It's the first time Joe's seen someone taller than himself and the first time "Smitty" has seen anyone even close to his height. They glare at each other and don't shake hands.

"Let the competition begin," Smitty whispers to Joe.

Gene smiles at the interaction as he blows his whistle. Bill Wheatley, 27, 6'4"; Francis Johnson, 26, 6'1"; Jack Ragland, 30, 6'1"; and "Tex" Gibbons, 28, 6'2" stop their workout and check out the new guy, Joe. They whistle and make catcalls. Joe knows he has to prove his worth to them. It's all part of being on a team. You have to bring value and Joe hopes he will fit in. He wants this job at the Refinery. It will be more money for the family, and he really wants to work with Gene Johnson, the top basketball coach of the day.

"Boys, this is Joe Fortenberry from Happy, Texas, and he went to West Texas State Teachers College. Joe, I think you've already seen Willard Schmidt. We call him Smitty. He's from Swanson, Nebraska, and went to Creighton." Joe and Smitty glare at each other again.

The coach continues, "Most of the team is from Kansas. Our captain, Bill Wheatley, is a farmer from Gypsum. He's studious and always has a book in his hand. Here's guard Jack Ragland, from Wichita and Wichita State, my brother, Francis, also from Wichita State, who's known for his steals. We grew up in Hartford. Here's a fellow Texan from Stratford and Southwestern College, forward "Tex" Gibbons." Each team member acknowledges him, but Joe knows it's all formality and he has to prove himself.

Gene says, "Now that the introductions are over, Francis, please demonstrate how the Refiner team steals." Francis, Jack, and Tex execute a fast and precise 2-on-1 play. Joe sees that the bar is set very high for this team.

Gene orders, "We're the Refiners and we're here to win. Let's get to work!" He blows the whistle again and Smitty tries to knock Joe off his balance. Throughout the drills, Smitty tries to intimidate Joe. Finally, Joe gets so angry that he does the unthinkable. He leaps and exposes his flashy, ungentlemanly, and undignified dunk. Gene immediately blows his whistle. The team stops, not at the whistle, but in amazement at the shot!

Joe looks at the coach with eyes that beg for forgiveness and says, "Sorry, Coach. I won't do it again. Sometimes I get carried away. I know the shot is too flashy, ungentlemanly, and undignified, and not worthy of the game."

"Are you kidding me? On this team you can be as flashy, ungentlemanly, and undignified as you want. That's the most exciting shot I've ever seen. Let's see it again." Relieved and exhilarated, Joe complies, and the rest of the players try unsuccessfully to make the shot. Even Smitty can't do it. Joe could jump eighteen inches off the floor easily and Smitty would have to practice and practice to jump more than four inches to compete with Joe.

Gene brags, "Boys, we're going to change the game!"

Smitty and the team surround Joe, congratulate him, and make him feel welcome.

Then Smitty says, "Just so you know, we're roommates on the road. I always get the new guy. But this time, I have the star! I'm rooting for you, buddy. Let's win!"

"Deal!" Joe answers. Smitty and Joe go under the basket and Joe teaches him the dunk.

CHAPTER 13

PHOG, MAUDE, AND THE UNIVERSALS

Inside the Kansas University training room, Phog observes as Naismith completes a chiropractic adjustment on John McLendon. Naismith cracks McLendon's back and says, "I've won more games off the court than on."

Phog replies, "Your sports medicine changed all athletics. Saved me many a game. That's for sure."

John rubs his lower back and comments, "Much better. Thank you. I'll think again before I scrimmage with a team again. They're too big and rough for me."

Naismith hands him an ice pack and says, "Apply this every hour for twenty minutes throughout the evening. You'll be good as new tomorrow."

"Yes, sir," John answers. As he leaves, Phog gently closes the door. Naismith sits, waiting to hear the complaint.

"That damned Gene Johnson and his evil fast break. He's changing the whole game with his "fire alarm, harem scarem" style. It causes excessive physical stress."

"It's two very tall men running fast at one player like there's a fire. Do that with another two men, and it's enough to "harem scarem" anyone. The game is evolving. Like a teenager coming into their own."

Phog slumps in a chair, aware that maybe he's out-with-the-old. Soon he bounces back in full Phog form by thinking of his next topic with Naismith.

"I'm begging you to go to the Olympics and be the basketball spokesman. We want to honor you as the inventor of the game."

"Phog, I was just foreclosed on my house and I'm on the Chautauqua Speech Tour for extra money. I can't go to Berlin."

Phog counters with I-won't-take-no-for-an-answer authority. "Since this is the first time basketball is being played as a full sport, the inventor of the game should be there."

"I'll speak to Maude," Naismith says.

Phog quickly blurts, "We'll raise the money for you both, but you have to promise me you'll go."

"If you can raise the money, Maude and I will do it," Naismith agrees.

★ ★ ★

A soft breeze rustles the delicate lace curtains of the Naismiths' bedroom. The floral wallpaper seems to envelope the couple as they pillow-talk in bed. After 40 years of marriage, they're still in love. Naismith faces Maude so she can read his lips.

"Darling, I want to make it up to you about foreclosing on the house."

"The kids are grown. We don't need such a big house."

"Phog wants us to be in Berlin for the Olympics. He'll raise the money. Wouldn't that be fun?"

"No. Too many crowds of people. I'll only hold you back. You go."

Naismith leans toward her romantically, "It could be a second honeymoon. First, we'd go to Scotland and stay with my family." Maude cuddles up to him and purrs, "I've always wanted to meet that part of your clan."

He responds by kissing her all over while he speaks, "It would be an adventure. All expenses paid. See Europe. Walk along the coast."

Maude lovingly responds, "You're irresistible. I would love to do all that. Of course, we'll go."

They kiss passionately as he slides his hands under her nightie.

The next night at the McPherson gym, the stands are packed with cute girls, Refiner V.I.P.s, and Naismith. There are banners, a band, and the press. All are expecting a great game between the harem-scarem Globe Refiners and the methodical Hollywood Universals.

As the crowd settles, the lights dim, and 26-year-old 6′7″ U.C.L.A. graduate Frank Lubin appears dressed as Frankenstein. The crowd screams as he parades around the gym and makes surprise, scary moves for the fans. When he departs, the rest of the Universals warm up (Sam Balter, age 26, 5′10″, from U.C.L.A.; Lloyd Goldstein, age 28, 6′0″, West Virginia; Carl Knowles, age 26, 6′2″ from U.C.L.A; Art Mollner, age 23, 6′0″ from Los Angeles City College; and Carl Shy, age 27, 6′0″, from U.C.L.A.). Lubin quickly disappears and later reappears in his basketball uniform to warm up as well. On the other side of the court, the Refiners limber up.

Quigley referees the game. Joe and Lubin leap for the tip-off, and Joe wins. Both teams play rough man-to-man, and at the half the Universals are up 20-15. Frustrated Refiner fans boo and throw popcorn at the team. The second half is a different story. Gene's strategy is to play "possum." Let the other team think the Refiners are asleep, then fast break.

Gene motions for a time-out and yells, "Time!" The team huddles.

Then Gene asks, "Tired of dribbling?"

The Refiners respond with a whole hearted, "Yes!"

Gene continues, "Ready to show them how we play basketball?"

"Ready!" The Refiners yell back.

"They're slow and plodding. Just run them to death."

Gene nods to team captain Bill Wheatley. Wheatley eyes the team and confidently orders, "Let's go get 'em."

Anytime the team hears "Let's go get 'em" from Bill Wheatley, they react like a fire truck on the way to a fire with the 2-2-1 fast break, harem-scarem. The play goes like this. Joe tips the ball to Tex. As the team runs toward the goal, Tex passes the ball to Francis, who is already under the net and easily makes a basket.

The next 17 points give the fans what they came to see, exciting basketball! The Refiners win 48-38. Naismith, Phog, McLendon, and O'shaughnessy are ecstatic and hurry to congratulate the team. The Universals are exhausted and flabbergasted.

When the Refiners see Naismith coming toward them, they surround him, and Naismith says admiringly, "No doubt, boys. Keep playing like this, and you're going to the Olympics."

CHAPTER 14

AVERY BRUNDAGE
AND THE BERLIN CONNECTION

In New York City, Olympic paraphernalia adorns the upscale office of enthusiastic and athletic Avery Brundage. He's a man of ego and power, and he loves controlling whatever comes his way. He even puffs on his cigar with authority.

Now he has to get rid of this pesky phone call and he blasts, "You tell him I'm the boss. Not only am I president of the American Olympic Committee, I'm president of the International Olympic Committee. I was in the Olympics, too, you know. Placed sixth in the 1912 Pentathalon. Now, good day!"

He hangs up the phone as Alexandra, his high-energy secretary rushes in. She's so efficient that she shortened her name to Alex just to save time. The lady is a New Yorker, period, complete with the accent and the determination. She's the first woman in her family to have a job in Manhattan, and she toils for long hours and little pay. But she's working for the American and International Olympic Committees and an authentic Olympic athlete! Enough said. As far as she's concerned, her star is rising.

She drops a set of papers on Brundage's desk and informs, "The Financial Coordinator is here."

As if on cue, Lyman Bingham huffs in, puts down his brief-case, and has a seat. No matter what his does, he seems to always have a cold. It's okay because he's a strategist. As long as he has a sharp mind, his blowing and sneezing can be forgiven. Also, he's old enough to be Avery's father and has a tendency to look after the kid. He rubs his balding head and prepares to speak as fast as he can.

Brundage has the first word. "Lyman, what's the good news?"

"New York to Berlin and back home on the luxurious *S.S. Manhattan!*" Lyman cheerily informs.

Brundage gives him a nod of approval. Lyman takes a deep breath and continues, "According to my calculations, our percentage of the basketball box office receipts and concessions at the Olympic Trials in Madison Square Garden will pay for all 400 athletes and staff at $500 a head." He quickly takes a breath and continues, "Food, lodging and transportation for five weeks, $200,000. However, there's no guarantee." Lyman holds his breath, then releases it with relief. He actually got to say everything he needed to without being interrupted.

Brundage, impressed, strolls to his window that overlooks the Hudson River and says, "The *S.S. Manhattan!* A luxury ship. Good work, Lyman."

"Yes, sir," Lyman acknowledges but is careful not to gloat. He knows the consequences of being too smug with Brundage.

"Now, we have to make sure the stands are packed and the people are hungry," Brundage laughs.

Lyman laughs with him and shifts in his seat. Now he's able to relax somewhat. Brundage continues, "Have the planning committee set up the dates and advertising." With that said, Lyman grabs his briefcase and Brundage waves him out.

Alex hurries in frantically. "Sir, sorry to interrupt, but Long Island University is refusing to play in the Olympic Trials at Madison Square Garden."

"And why not?" Brundage wonders.

Alex reads from her notes, "Long Island University, on principle, will participate in no way, shape or form with the Hitler games."

Brundage scoffs, "Hitler." Annoyed he continues, "Tell the "un-American, alien agitators" at Long Island University that I'm going to Berlin myself with an interpreter! I'll see if there will be discrimination to our Jews or Negroes."

"Yes, sir," Alex says as she quickly leaves.

Raging, Brundage paces, puffing on his cigar.

In Berlin, Brundage and drinking buddy/interpreter Ritter Van Holt are whisked away in a chauffeur-driven Mercedes limousine. An intimidating S.S. chaperone accompanies them. The well-equipped bar has beer, wine, and hard liquor with cheese, sausages, and pickles.

The chaperone offers, "Please partake in our finest cheeses and beers."

Van Holt, a man who doesn't turn down anything but his collar lunges for a beer and some pickles, saying, "I don't mind if I do."

"Thank you," Brundage replies. The two men sit back munching and drinking as they view the streets of Berlin. The route has been carefully designed to show Germany at its best. It's almost creepy, it's so perfect. All the houses have fresh paint and red geraniums are in every window box. They look further down the street and see JEWS VERBOTEN signs. The men exchange a concerned look. This is what they were afraid of: Germany wasn't as it seemed.

At Goebbels' palatial office, the chaperone, Goebbels, Brundage, and Van Holt convene. The office is very ornate and meant to intimidate. A silver tray with a crystal water pitcher and crystal glasses is in the center of the perfectly polished table.

Goebbels is in charge and says, "We've created jobs, prestige, and work ethic among our happy people."

Brundage replies, "Even though I'm an admirer of Nazi Germany, this issue just won't go away. The world sees the Fuhrer failing as an Olympic host."

Goebbels glares at him. Cool Brundage glares back.

Van Holt tries to lighten the mood and speaks in German, "We're here to exchange ideas."

Goebbels gives Van Holt a "don't patronize me" look.

Then Goebbels asks Brundage, "Isn't it true that you belong to a gentlemen's club that doesn't allow Jews or Negroes?"

"Yes, of course, but this is the Olympic Games. There can be no discrimination."

Brundage reaches for water. The chaperone pours it for him. He also pours a glass for Van Holt and places it before him.

Goebbels inquires, "How does your President Roosevelt stand?"

"He's neutral, sir. Germany's laws are for the German people." Brundage sips the water and maintains his composure, then continues, "The International Olympic Committee's rules are for the Olympics only. The world must know that all athletes will be safe." Goebbels and Brundage lock eyes. Van Holt nervously reaches for his water.

After an intense moment, Goebbels stands to leave and says, "You can assure the International Olympic Committee that all athletes will be safe. Our image is of utmost importance to us."

Brundage stands, extends his hand and says, "Then it's done. I'll get the paperwork to you this afternoon." They shake on it. Goebbels walks out, his dignity intact.

The next day, Brundage and Van Holt are escorted to the airport in the sleek limo. In the background, the JEWS VERBOTEN signs have been removed. Brundage and Van Holt see this and exchange a confident look. After the limo passes, the signs are returned.

Back in New York, Brundage is behind a table of microphones for a press conference. He wears a light tan suit and is impeccably coifed.

Not a hair is out of place. His decision about America going to the Berlin Olympics has been greatly anticipated. Cameras roll and flashbulbs pop. Phog Allen is among the crowd waiting with anticipation. Brundage seizes the moment. He knows he has a trapped audience. He sits at the center microphone with his speech in his hands with all the poise of an Olympic athlete ready to win. He takes a moment, spots Phog, and reads.

"I have determined after my travels to Berlin, that Germany is fit to have the Olympics." There are some boos from the crowd. Brundage smoothly continues, "The games are for the people, not politicians. This is nothing more than a communist conspiracy to keep America out of the games. I encourage all American athletes to put representing their country above all else. Speaking for the American Olympic Committee, I can say that there will be teams representing the United States in the 1936 games."

The crowd applauds and rushes toward him. Police hold the people back. Brundage gets up and shakes hands with some of the onlookers. He looks for Phog, and when he sees him, he reaches out and they vigorously shake hands.

Meanwhile, at the McPherson Gym, the Refiners huddle around the radio to listen to Brundage's press conference. In the background is the constant clanking of the refinery. They all wonder if that sound is their fate for the rest of their lives, or are they going to Berlin, on an adventure of a lifetime?

When they hear Brundage say that America will be at the Games, Gene doesn't waste any time and barks, "Team, you heard him. America's going to the Olympics. Get serious if you want to go to Berlin." Gene blows his whistle and the team huddles.

Gene says, "If we're going to win the Olympic gold, we have to win the A.A.U. championship first." Each team member stares at Gene with fierce determination. It's so extreme that Bill Wheatley breaks the tension with, "Let's go get 'em." The team laughs. Gene blows his whistle and the team gets to work.

In the next months, the Refiners win every A.A.U. game. They stomp the Universals, give autographs, and take photos with movie stars. These guys are having the time of their lives. Nothing like partying at the Brown Derby and having lots of fun with plenty of liquor and loose women.

CHAPTER 15

REALITY

Back home in the refinery classroom, charts about shale and oil samples cover the four walls. An instructor points to examples as he speaks of them. The basketball team tries to stay awake.

Droning on, the instructor says, "The purpose of a refinery is to separate crude oil into useful products. Petroleum, naphtha, gasoline, diesel fuel, asphalt base, heating oil, kerosene, and liquefied petroleum gas." Francis nods off. Smitty snores. Bill shakes Smitty.

The instructor hears the snore, turns, and says, "Boys, you need to show an interest in your job. Be prepared in case you get a chance to work here after the Olympics!"

Joe comes to life first and answers, "Yes, sir."

"We won the game last night then went to celebrate," Bill adds.

"And where was this celebration?" the instructor wants to know.

Francis says, "Uncle Lou's Barbershop and Pool Hall. My grandma was there. She runs it."

Jack mentions, "Francis beat every pool challenger."

The instructor acts a bit dumbfounded, "Does your brother, I mean your coach, know about this?"

"Of course. He's the one that taught me how to hustle pool," Francis laughs.

Frustrated, the instructor puts on his jacket and says, "I give up. Clearly you're not that interested in gasoline."

"We're interested in all minerals that come from the ground," Smitty teases.

Bill laughs, "Especially gold!" The guys all hoot with him.

The instructor motions for them to leave and says, "Get out of here and win tonight!"

The team exits together and chants, "We will! We're unbeatable!"

Valentine's Day, Friday, February 14, 1936 turns out to be quite memorable for the Refiners. At the McPherson High School band practice room, charismatic August San Romani conducts his uniformed band in a Refiners victory song. Howie, the band's first-chair brass player, has his bugle ready.

August encourages the band, "Magnifico! You will help the team win and the stands will go wild, wild, wild!"

"Only because your bands win every championship west of the Mississippi, Mr. San Romani," Howie says with a wink and a smile.

"Grazie. Grazie. Now, line up. We have a separate bus. Tubas first." They all stand and after Howie toots the bugle call, the band heads for their bus.

In the McPherson High School parking lot, 200 freezing-cold people vie for seating on four busses to go see the Refiners stomp the Santa Fe Trailers. I. A. O'shaughnessy and Phog observe the crowd from I. A.'s Cadillac.

Phog says, "Excellent. With these kinds of crowds, we'll make enough to get Dr. Naismith to the Olympics."

"Ticket sales are brisk. You'd never know there was a Depression," I. A. mentions as he motions for his driver to head on out. The Cadillac leads the caravan of busses and cars, all with their front lights blazing in broad daylight. They pass wheat farms and undulating hills as they head toward the Kansas City Armory.

At the armory gym, the Refiner fans arrive and hurry to their seats. Before the game, Phog and I. A. shake hands with the team and wish them well. Naismith arrives with John McLendon, and Naismith motions for the men to circle him.

Starting to pray, Naismith bows his head. The team follows. "On this blessed night, may the Lord bless and keep you. Play fair, play courteously, yet play to win. Mind, Body, Spirit! Amen." The team adds an "Amen," and the players sprint to their positions on the court.

It's a routine game but the Refiners are down at the half, 16-15. In the locker room, Gene is anything but quiet. He paces angrily.

"I don't believe you. One point. You're behind one point! You're out of step. Your entire rhythm is off. Let's put this to bed. Are you a team? Ragland, where were you? You're supposed to cover for Tex since his dad died."

Tex says, "Coach, my dad wanted to be here tonight and he would want me to be here too. I'm okay."

Gene adds, "Have compassion. Win for his dad." Trying to hold back the tears, Tex covers his head with a towel. Jack and the rest of the team lower their heads.

Out of patience, Gene yells, "And Wheatley, you've been off all night. Joe gets the tip and where are you boys? You let the other team dive on the ball. Do you want to go to the A.A.U. Nationals? No Nationals, no Olympics. Do you want to go to Berlin?"

"Yes!" The team answers. "Yes!"

"I didn't hear you," Gene shouts.

"Yes!" The team yells back. They rally and are fired up to win.

In the third quarter, two Trailers, Ray Piper and Herman Fischer, dramatize their injuries to outfox the Refiners.

Gene huddles with the players. "Okay, team," he says. "Ray Piper has a sprained knee and Fischer has a torn ligament. But don't let them fool you. Harem-scarem and let's win this thing now." Gene puts his hand in and the team joins him.

Bill commands, "Let's go get 'em!"

The Refiners return to the court. The crowd is anxious and wild foot stamping begins. The fire truck 2-2-1 strategy works and the Refiners eliminate the Trailers' eight-point lead in the last three minutes of play. Score: 38 to 37. Naismith, McLendon, Phog Allen, and I. A. are on the edge of their seats. The exhausted teams seesaw to and fro. The last center jump (jump ball) is controlled by Joe, but the Trailers smother it before the tying shot can be launched. The Refiners lose 44-42. The fans, along with Howie and the band, drag themselves to the busses for a very long ride home.

CHAPTER 16

HITLER VS. JEWS, BLACKS, AND WOMEN

With a fire burning in the fireplace, Hitler's office is warm and cozy. Hitler is busy signing various papers that Goebbels has given him, and he seems to be in a good mood.

When the moment is right, Goebbels says, "There's something else to discuss, Fuhrer."

Hitler looks up from his work and asks, "What is it?"

"The International Olympic Committee insists that Germany has Jews competing in the Olympics or we'll be boycotted."

Outraged, Hitler throws the papers at Goebbels, saying, "I don't even want this Jewish, Negro fest."

Goebbels patiently collects the papers and says, "I must emphasize, it's a good way to show our Aryan superiority. How can they ever win?"

"They can't win. We'll pay someone off to lose. I'm sure the Jews can be bought," Hitler sneers.

Goebbels laughs, "Let's just threaten them. That will save money."

Hitler laughs with him and says, "Tell them we will kill their families if they refuse to follow our rules." They laugh together, knowing that the plan to exterminate the Jews is well under way.

Hitler reaches into the top drawer of his desk and says, "Here's the signatures for the prostitutes. All beautiful Aryans."

"Yes, Fuhrer. They will be kept in a separate section called the Love Garden, a free, bawdy, yet opulent, whorehouse with every ploy, toy, or position a man could desire."

"Excellent!" Hitler says, "It's the women's job to exhaust the foreign athletes. That way, Germany has a chance to win more medals. Let them know up front that we'll pay for pregnancies. But only, if they have a card saying they're part of this elite corps. Make it seem like a national honor."

Goebbels agrees and with a devilish smirk says, "Good. We'll dominate the games in every way. A triumph of the Aryan race and Nazi Germany." He extends his arm and says, "Sieg Heil." Then Goebbels takes the necessary paperwork and exits. Hitler saunters to the window, admires the view, and watches his Hitler Youth marching.

Figure 1. *James Naismith with his sister, Annie, and little brother Robbie, 1868.*

Figure 2. *McGill University graduation, 1890.*

Figure 3. *Y.M.C.A. Springfield, Massachusetts, 1891.*

Figure 4. *Original Springfield, Massachusetts, Y.M.C.A. gymnasium, 2017.*

Figure 5. *Y.M.C.A. Emblem designed by Luther Gulick, Naismith's boss.*

Figure 6. *Y.M.C.A gymnasium, 1891.*

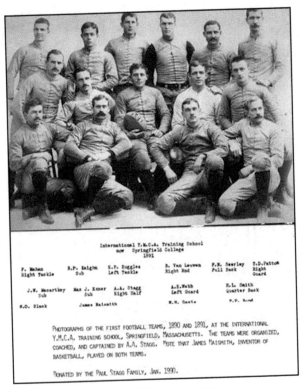

Figure 7. *15 of the 18 Incorrigibles, 1891.*
Naismith was on the team but is not shown in this photo.

Figure 8. *Maude, 1890s.*

Figure 9. *The Naismiths' Springfield, Massachusetts, home.*

Figure 10. *Naismith with ball and peach basket.*

Figure 11. *Referee "Quig" Quigley, shown here in his other job as a baseball umpire.*

Figure 12. *"Phog" Allen, the father of basketball coaching.*

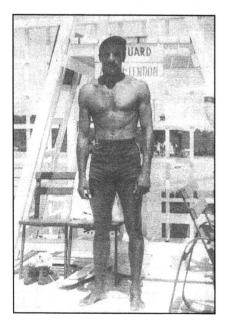

Figure 13. *John McLendon as a lifeguard, 1932.*

Figure 14. *John McLendon, the father of basketball integration.*

Figure 15. *Joe Fortenberry, the first "big man" in nasketball and inventor of the slam dunk.*

Figure 16. *Joe Fortenberry boxing.*

Figure 17. *The Fortenberry family—Joe is fourth from the right.*

Figure 18. *Globe Oil Refinery, McPherson, Kansas, in—1932.*

Figure 19. *Globe Oil Refinery signage.*

Figure 20. *Globe Oil Refiners team jacket.*

Figure 21. *McPherson gym, 1932.*

Figure 22. *Refiners basketball program, 1934.*

C
O
P
Y

June 1, 1934

Mr. Gene Johnson
McPherson, Kansas

Dear Mr. Johnson:

Referring to our several conversations which we have had in my office, and your proposal of April 15 addressed to Mr. F.L. Jehle, with respect to our company sponsoring a basketball team during the coming season.

Our company would be willing to sponsor such a team to be managed by you under the following conditions:

We will give you $1,500 with which to operate the team and to compensate you for your work. You are to assume full responsibility for promoting and financing the team for the entire season, and no other expense shall attach to our company in connection with the matter, except the employment of, and compensation to the players involved. Should you succeed in winning the national championship, it would be agreable upon our part to give you a bonus of not less than $500.

It is our understanding that it will be your own responsibility to provide practice court, supply shoes, balls, etc. Should you find it necessary, it will be agreeable upon our part to purchase the necessary balls, shoes, etc. at the beginning of the season, however, the charge for same will be applied against the total of $1,500 which you are to receive. The sum of $1,500 less any advances upon our part in connection with the purchase of playing equipment and miscellaneous supplies, will be made to you in equal monthly installments beginning November 1, 1934.

You have represented to us that it probably will be possible for you to secure outstanding players such as Fortenberry, Colvin, Deitz, Ragland, Vaughn, Johnson, Gibbon and several others, in view of which we shall expect you to procure the services of at least a majority of the players mentioned.

It is our understanding that the matter of financing games, both at home and abroad, will be your own responsibility, and that no liability in this connection will attach to our company, other than your agreed compensation heretofore indicated.

Figure 23. *Gene Johnson coaching contract, 1934.*

```
                                              C
                                               O
                                               P
                                                Y


Mr. Gene Johnson - 2                                    June 1, 1934


        I shall treat the matter of employment of, and compensation
for such employment of the players in another letter.

        Your signed acceptance to this letter will serve as the
agreement between yourself and our company in connection with the
matter.

                        Very truly yours,

                        THE GLOBE OIL & REFINING COMPANY


                        By_____A. E. Landsittel_____ (Signed)
                                   Sales Manager


ACCEPTED:


    Gene Johnson          (Signed)
```

Figure 23. *(continued).*

Figure 24. *The Universals, 1936.*

Figure 25. *The Universals' home court: the Shrine Auditorium, Los Angeles.*

Figure 26. *Make-up artist Jack Pierce and Frank Lubin as Frankenstein.*

Figure 27. *Willard Schmidt (left) and Joe Fortenberry (right) with Coach Johnson at Madison Square Garden, 1936.*

Figure 28. *Quig Quigley in action as a referee.*

Figure 29. *Refiners vs. Universals at the Olympic Trials in Madison Square Garden, 1936.*

Figure 30. *Willard Schmidt (left) and Joe Fortenberry (right) scrimmaging.*

SPORTS   THE NEW YORK TIMES, TUESDAY, MARCH 10, 1936.

Golden Gloves Finals Draw 20,000 Boxing Fans to Garden

SCALZO REGISTERS UPSET OVER COYLE

Thwarts Last Year's Rider of 112-Pound Class in Bid for Bantamweight Title.

MASILIGO WINS FAST BOUT

Gains 'Golden Gloves' Decision Over O'Brien—Cates and Howell Score Knockdowns.

U. S. Olympic Team Tops Champion British Sic, 6-3

KLING VANQUISHES APPLEBY BY 300-150

Upsala Farmer Champion in First Match of Amateur Title Billiard Play.

SOUSSA TOPS FESSENDER

VENZKE FIT TO RUN IN COLUMBIAN MILE

O'BRIEN IN THE CASEY 600

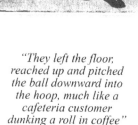

"They left the floor, reached up and pitched the ball downward into the hoop, much like a cafeteria customer dunking a roll in coffee"

Awesome Kansas Giants Reverse Basketball Lay-Up Shot Process

McPherson Oilers Leap and Hurl Ball Downward to Target, Disdaining Upward Tosses—Schmidt, 6 Feet 9, Tallest of Team in First Workout Here for Olympic Trials.

By ARTHUR J. DALEY.

The advance notices said that the Oilers of McPherson, Kan., were the tallest and best basketball team in the world. They arrived in New York yesterday for their game with Long Island University and assorted collegians at Madison Square Garden tomorrow and promptly proved the point as to their size. And after a workout at the West Side Y. M. C. A. they left observers convinced that perhaps the other statement was no exaggeration either.

First the Missouri Valley A. A. U. champions and No. 1 favorites for the American Olympic team berth practiced shooting. It became so monotonous that any throw that rolled off the hoop brought from the spectators an excited "Hey, that fellow just missed one."

Onlookers Are Surprised.

The McPherson version of a lay-up shot left observers simply flabbergasted. Joe Fortenberry, 6-foot 8-inch center, and Willard Schmidt, 6-foot 9-inch forward, did not use an ordinary curling toss. Not those giants. They left the floor, reached up and pitched the ball downward into the hoop, much like a cafeteria customer dunking a roll in coffee.

After that exhibition the Oilers staged a scrimmage, the first team against the second. The defense was what caused the most surprise. The two forwards raced around after the ball and left the other three to form a loose zone, but there was no dropping back to the center line and permitting rival offenses to form. Continual harrying of ball-handlers gave these tactics punch.

No team around here ever played at such breathless pace and with such furious drive as the Oilers. They never stop digging. Long passes, short passes, the pivot play, make them the scoring combination they are.

Coach Gene Johnson was asked how a good college team would fare against his McPherson quintet. To make the question a little more specific, he was queried as to how Notre Dame or Purdue, for instance, would do.

"We could spot either Notre Dame or Purdue 10 or 12 points," he said crisply. "And that's not my own opinion, either. Competent basketball men have told me the same thing."

Plenty of Action Ahead.

At that rate the all-metropolitan collegians are in for a mighty eventful evening, even though Coach Clair Bee probably will use as a unit his thirty-three straight. He will need the ample reinforcements of other collegians, because the Oilers would wear down a single team in no time.

Before the scrimmage Coach Johnson instructed the referee. "Call all the fouls you can find," he ordered, "because we want to find what we can get away with around here."

Word had reached New York that the McPherson record in the very testing competition of the Missouri Valley A. A. U. had been twelve victories and four defeats. Johnson was queried as to what the Oiler total record was.

"I forget exactly," he said, "but those four games were the only ones we lost. We've played about thirty-five."

Mite Among Giants.

Ten men made the trip. The Oilers even brought along their lone "midget," Dave Petre, who is only 5 feet 10 inches tall. But Petre is supposed to make 80 per cent of his set shots. He made four of five in the last two minutes of one game to save the day for the Oilers.

The first team that was used yesterday in practice averaged 6 feet 6½ inches in height, but the usual starting five averages only 6 feet 4½. Schmidt is the tallest at 6:9. Then come Fortenberry, 6:8; Harry Dowd, 6:6; Vernon Vaughn, 6:5; Bill Wheatly, 6:4; Tex Gibbons, 6:2; Francis Johnson, Jack Ragland and Charles Bailey, 6:1 each and Petre, 5:10.

Figure 31. New York Times *article proving the origin of the slam dunk, 1936.*

The victorious Universals being congratu-
lated by studio chief Carl Laemmle, Sr.

Courtesy of Universal Studios.

Figure 32. *Carl Laemmle accepts the trophy for the Universals'*
Olympic Trials win, 1936.

ROXY THEATRES CORPORATION
133 WEST 50TH STREET
NEW YORK

August 28, 1936.

HOWARD S. CULLMAN

of the

ROXY THEATRE

Cordially invites the

Members of the American Olympic Team

To be the guests

of the

Roxy Theatre

On Monday Afternoon, August 31st, 1936

※※※※※※

This letter admits One (1).
Please present it at the
EXECUTIVE ENTRANCE,
Located at #133 West 50th Street.

#------

Figure 33. *Roxy Theater invitation, 1936.*

Figure 34. *Hotel Lincoln after-game dine and dance invitation, 1936.*

Figure 35. *The* S.S. Manhattan.

Figure 36. *Joe Fortenberry's embarkation card.*

Figure 37. *U.S. Olympic Team on the* S.S. Manhattan.

Figure 38. *Jesse Owens demonstrating his skill on the* S.S. Manhattan.

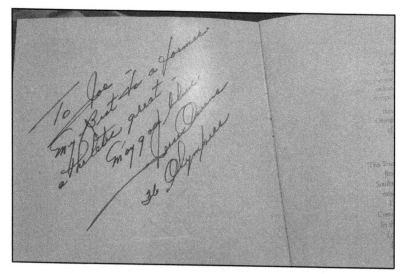

Figure 39. *Joe Fortenberry's Jesse Owens autograph.*

Figure 40. *The U.S. Olympic Team landing in Germany.*

Figure 41. *An Olympic Games poster.*

Figure 42. *Willard Schmidt, Frank Lubin, and Joe Fortenberry outside their cabin at the Olympic village.*

Figure 43. *Adolf Hitler and Leni Riefenstahl at the 1936 Olympics.*

Figure 44. *Leni Riefenstahl at work on her film* Olympia.

Figure 45. *The Olympic stadium.*

ADOLF HITLER

Figure 46. *Hitler officially opening the Olympic Games.*

Figure 47. *The 1936 U.S. Olympic Team entering the stadium during opening ceremony.*

Figure 48. *The torch bearer enters.*

Figure 49. *Hitler at the Olympics.*

Figure 50. *The stadium crowd saluting Hitler.*

Figure 51. *Jesse Owens' broad jump and the medal ceremony.*

Figure 52. *The Berg ball, palmed by Jimmy Steward, son of the silver medalist of the same name. (Courtesy of the* Windsor Star.*)*

Figure 53. *Philippines vs. Estonia and Poland vs. Latvia at the Olympic Games, 1936.*

Figure 54. *Philippines vs. Mexico. Mexico won the bronze.*

Figure 55. *The final game, US vs. Canada. Joe Fortenberry (12) blocks a shot.*
America beats Canad 19-8 and wins the gold!

Figure 56. *Joe Fortenberry's 1936 Olympic gold medal.*

Figure 57. *James Naismith presents the first Olympic gold medal in basketball to Bill Wheatley. Joe Fortenberry second from the left.*

A Message from Mayor LaGuardia to the Members of the American Olympic Team returning on the President Roosevelt:

The Mayor's Committee of Welcome has made complete arrangements to provide for your comfort, entertainment and enjoyment from the hour of your arrival in New York Harbor to the grand climax of New York City's reception and welcome to all the returning Olympic athletes on Thursday, September third.

On September third, an old-fashioned ticker-tape parade up Broadway from the Battery to Harlem will give New York's millions an opportunity to express their pride and joy over the great achievements of America's participants in the 1936 Olympic Games.

At one o'clock the Mayor will provide a luncheon for the City's guests to be held at New York's new municipal stadium at Randall's Island.

Immediately after luncheon the City of New York will bestow commemorative medals not only upon each of the point winners in the 1936 Olympics but upon each of the participants.

In the presentation of these attractive medals, each bearing the name of the recipient and carrying on one side the Seal of the City of New York and on the other side the original Olympian symbol of victory, the Mayor will be assisted by world-famous old timers in the field of sport, heroes of days gone by, such as:

JACK DEMPSEY
BENNY LEONARD
JACK CURLEY
BILL ROBINSON
PAUL PILGRIM
PAT McDONALD
CHICK MEEHAN
"RED" BURMAN
MICKEY WALKER
JACK JOHNSON
FRANK KRAMER
FRED SPENCER
GERTRUDE EDERLE
EILEEN RIGGIN

BABE RUTH
VINCENT RICHARDS
JOHNNY DUNDEE
MAUREEN ORCUTT (Crews)
JOHN FLANAGAN
JIMMY BRADDOCK
LOU LITTLE
MATT McGRATH
GENE TUNNEY
MEL SHEPPARD
PHILADELPHIA JACK O'BRIEN
PERRY CHARLES
LOU HANDLEY
EARL SANDE

SAM LANGFORD

This presentation ceremony will be broadcast to your own home town so that your relatives and friends can listen in through arrangements made with three major networks, NBC, CBS and MBS.

In the evening you will be the guests of the Mayor's Committee at one of America's famous supper theatres, the French Casino, for a brand new show which has just opened.

During the five days intervening between your arrival here and the monster reception on September third, you will not only have a key to the heart of the City of New York, but you will be provided with rooms, meals, transportation and entertainment of every variety, during each day and evening, without any cost to yourselves.

A more detailed schedule of events and entertainment will be included in your copy of the souvenir program presented by the Mayor's Committee.

Figure 58. *Flyer explaining the monster ticker-tape parade planned for the return of the 1936 Olympic athletes.*

Figure 59. *Naismith and Maude at home.*

CHAPTER 17

PRIDE AND THE SLAM DUNK

At another practice scrimmage at the McPherson gym, a sad Joe Fortenberry is wearing street clothes on the sidelines. Francis and Bill wear gym clothes but they're benched. Smitty and Tex score to end the practice. Gene dashes for the locker room. The always-present reporters surround him and one says, "Coach, you didn't play your brother in most of the practice and Joe Fortenberry is in street clothes. Care to comment?"

Gene replies, "We're trying some new strategies, and Joe, well, he lost his uniform."

"Looks like punishment to me. Joe's not one to lose his uniform."

Gene grimaces and says, "Just making sure our priorities are straight. We don't slack off in training and we're compassionate with team members. We win in basketball, but we don't brag about it, and we're attentive to the day job as well."

"Ugh hum," the reporter mumbles knowing Gene is up to something.

"I can't make the boys train. But I can sure make them want to train, or it's the bench. As the great James Naismith said, basketball is about developing the character in men."

The reporter looks up from his busy notetaking and asks, "What's next, Coach?"

"Exhibition game, Madison Square Garden, The best of the West versus the East Coast Ivy Leaguers. Just think of the publicity." He nudges the reporter, and the reporter is all smiles because he knows he just might get a juicy quote or an exclusive story from Gene.

★ ★ ★

In New York City, the Refiners are living it up again. They see sites such as the Empire State Building, Broadway, the subway, and the automat, just to name a few. Reporters and sexually available groupies follow them everywhere.

At Dempsey's, the team enjoys a sumptuous meal. Plenty of ladies flirt with them and successful men admire them. The master of ceremonies steps up to the microphone. Gene leans toward the team and says, "Bottoms up, boys. We have to get up early tomorrow."

As the team finishes their drinks, the master of ceremonies announces, "Ladies and gentlemen, before they leave, I'd like to introduce our special guests this evening. You've seen them in the newsreels. You've read about them in the papers. It's the world's tallest basketball team: the Globe Refiners." The patrons rise to give them a standing ovation. The team stands to acknowledge their applause and towers over them. The patrons are stunned. They've never seen men that tall before. As they leave, the team signs autographs and shakes hands from table to table. The patrons are still in awe after they leave.

★ ★ ★

The next day, Joe and Smitty rubberneck down the street with the rest of the team. Even in their dapper outfits, they seem out of place. Some blasé New Yorkers glance and notice their height, then quickly move on. The squad goes into an automat for lunch. Joe and Smitty take off for the restroom. They see the row of stalls and notice that it's a pay-toilet. Both check their pockets. No coins. They look at each other and shrug. Together they reach over their stall door, unlatch the hook, and proceed to use the facilities. When other patrons come in, they see Joe and Smitty's heads high above the stalls. Some walk back out, and others try not to stare and wait respectfully for a turn.

That evening the Refiners arrive at Madison Square Garden. Angry people who want America to boycott the Olympics carry signs and try to block the door. Police escort the Refiners inside.

Bill, Joe, and Smitty don't have to duck to get through this doorway. They're dumbfounded by the huge space.

Smitty whistles to see if there is an echo and there is! It's soft and eerie.

Bill asks, "I wonder how many bales of hay this could hold?"

Joe and Smitty turn to him and Smitty remarks, "What's the saying? You can take the boy out of the farm, but—" Joe finishes the sentence, saying, "you can't take the farm out of the boy".

Bill laughs and takes off for the locker room. Joe and Smitty follow him.

Later, the East and West exhibition teams warm up on opposite ends of the court. The College All-Stars, none of whom are Jewish, impress with their drills and skills. Joe starts with his long shots from 25 feet away and the crowd of 7,000 goes wild. Naismith, Phog, and the two referees, Quig Quigley and Alvin Bell, wait beside the press box and a quickly set-up microphone.

Naismith watches Joe and says to Phog, "This is the future of basketball."

Phog refers to the crowd and answers, "They won't believe what they're going to see tonight." The men smile with knowledge and continue to watch the team.

Their thoughts are interrupted when "The Star-Spangled Banner" is played with gusto. After, Naismith takes the microphone for opening words and a prayer.

He says, "In these trying times, it's even more important to play fair and enjoy the game. I firmly believe that a world that plays together, stays together. Let us pray...." All heads are bowed as he recites the Lord's Prayer.

★ ★ ★

In the game, the Eastern style of patterned defense, precise dribbling, and accurate passing of the All-Stars contrasts with the fire alarm, harem-scarem attack of the Refiners. The All-Stars' Coach, Clair Bee, later to be inducted into the Naismith Memorial Basketball Hall of Fame, and his assistant watch as Joe and Smitty continually jump up and bat the ball away from the goal. When the Refiners score with another lay-up, Coach Bee signals a time-out to referee Quig Quigley.

The All-Stars huddle with Bee and he says, "Those tall guys are hitting the ball away every time it gets close to a basket. You have to arc the ball over so they can't get at it. Stay on them man-to-man," Coach Bee orders. The All-Stars head for the court and prepares for a systematic defense.

Coach Bee turns to his assistant and asks, "What have you got?"

"They fall behind early and stage a furious comeback," he answers.

Frustrated, Coach Bee spews, "I know that! Give me something new."

"Then they hold on for dear life."

Coach Bee suddenly gets an idea and says, "We have to stop that *dear life* right now!" They're interrupted when the game resumes and an All-Star fouls.

Quig immediately blows his whistle and starts running down the court, yelling his popular phrase, "You can't dooooo that!"

The crowd responds, "You can't dooooo that!" Mimicking that phrase was something the crowd looked forward to at each game Quig refereed.

Coach Bee has no time to enjoy the game, Quig, or the crowd. Now he calls another time-out. His team rushes in. He commands, "Shoot as often as you can. You have to squash them like annoying ants." Overwhelmed, the All-Stars return to the game.

Coach Bee yells from the side, "Shoot the works. Shoot the works!"

The All-Stars make many of their long shots. They're so good that after numerous rough-and-tumble fouls on both sides, Gene explodes in Alvin Bell's face, "What the hell? You let the defense get away with murder but soak the offense if they touch a man. I'm reporting you!"

Mercifully, the half-time clock buzzes. The All-Stars lead by 13 points. Score: 25 to 12. Gene Johnson is livid. He and the team head for the locker room.

Reporters surround the angry Coach Johnson. An aggressive *New York Post* reporter pushes his way forward and asks, "Some skeptics are saying your Kansas Skyscrapers can't keep up the pace for 40 minutes against the best New York college boys. Is that true?"

Gene pivots and graciously evades the question by saying, "You have the best bunch of shooters I've ever seen."

The *Post* reporter smiles as he jots down notes. Gene continues, "Hank Luisetti's one-handers are tops." Now the *Post* reporter is really smiling.

"But if we can't beat a bunch of college guys, then I'm a very, very bad coach!" The other reporters whoop and holler and the *New York Post* reporter is deflated.

Gene disappears to the locker room, knowing he has fueled the fire. He has the reporters on his side. Now it was time to put on a show and win this game.

Midway through the last half, the Refiners trail 38-28. Gene calls in the team and says, "Ready to win this game?"

Bill Wheatley and the team nods "yes" to Gene. Then the team turns to Joe.

Gene says, "Ready, Joe? Ready to show them your invention?"

"Can't wait," Joe answers.

With that, Bill utters the magic words, "Let's go get 'em."

On command, the tandem team of Wheatley and Fortenberry lead the charge. Next is the most thrilling, fast, slow, reverse, then charge basketball New York has ever seen.

Arthur Daley, a young up-and-coming sports writer for *The New York Times* eagerly awaits on a press phone. He's surrounded by other frantic sports reporters as he relays play-by-play to his office.

It's business as usual. Coach Bee and Gene Johnson are yelling at the players and calling time-outs. The All-Stars rally until Bill Wheatley and Joe Fortenberry lead the harem- scarem. Suddenly, most of the Refiners are at the goal. The All-Stars wonder what is going on.

The frenzied crowd watches Bill passes the ball to Joe. He steps toward the net and jumps so high above the goal that he is able to slam the ball through the basket. The crowd is ecstatic! The Refiners are ecstatic!

Daley is beside himself and shouts, "Whoa! I've never seen anything like this. Big Joe Fortenberry belongs to the original Phi Slamma Jamma fraternity. On a run, he leaps above ten feet and he slams the ball downward into the hoop much like a cafeteria customer dunking a roll in coffee. I'm calling this shot a slam dunk!"

Joe slam-dunks again and the New York crowd goes even more crazy. Naismith and Phog cheer with them. The rest of the game is highlighted by the mesmerizing 2-2-1 zone defense and a spectacular play when Smitty runs and passes to Joe for another score. Their timing is impeccable and they know it. Bill scores on three rushes, and Francis intercepts and makes six of his seven shots. Joe taps in a miss for the Refiners' first lead: 43-42. The crowd is on their feet!

The *New York Post* reporter can't believe his eyes and yells into his phone, "The Empire State Building of the Refiners, Joe Fortenberry, just pulled this team into the lead. His hand and eye coordination is so strong, I've heard he can shoot a rabbit from a running horse."

Daley adds, "Ladies and Gentlemen, I'm watching the tallest, wildest, and best basketball team in the United States. Looks like it's all over for the All-Stars."

Indeed, it is. The end buzzer blasts and the Refiners win 45-43. Full of ecstasy, the team congratulates each other then heads for the locker room. The stunned crowd disperses. Reporters and avid fans try to surround Naismith and Phog, but they immediately disappear into the locker room.

As is the custom, the Refiners line up to greet Naismith.

Phog introduces them one by one, "and this is Joe Fortenberry."

"It's an honor to see you again, sir," Joe says.

"You're making history, young man. If I had known about you, I would have made the basket a foot higher," Naismith jokes.

"Thank you. Just trying my best."

Naismith adds, "Keep doing it! Keep doing it! You make the game exciting."

The next big showdown is the American Athletic Union Championship in Denver. The top two teams go on to the Olympic Trials at Madison Square Garden in April. There, they play the best university teams. The best two teams from this group combine and go to the Olympics in August.

CHAPTER 18

ABOUT MAUDE

An unusually tense John McLendon picks up Naismith from his trip to New York at the train station. As John begins to drive Naismith home, he mentions, "We'll take the short way today. Everyone is anxious to see you."

Naismith says, "Just as long as we see some hoops. It's my favorite scenery!"

They travel through streets, joyfully pointing to people playing basketball and spotting hoops on the sides of houses and barns, and in playgrounds.

Naismith chatters, "It was the most exciting play New York had ever seen. They named it the *slam dunk*. Now basketball has its own signature play, like a home run in baseball or a touchdown in football."

John pulls into Naismith's driveway and starts unloading his suitcases. Naismith jumps out of the car and spreads his arms as if to hug his house. He says, "Home sweet home!" John continues with the luggage, places it on the porch, and says, "I'll be at the next Refiners game. That's for sure."

"Thank you, John. Coming in?" Naismith asks.

"Not today. I have to study."

"Okay. See you in class."

"Glad to be of help, sir."

Naismith hurries into the house calling, "Dearie, I'm home. I'm home." Naismith hangs up his coat and starts toward the kitchen. "Dearie, oh Dearie, I have a present for you. A little Statue of Liberty and some good stories—"

Suddenly, the family physician, Dr. Strickland, emerges from the bedroom and Naismith freezes.

"I'm sorry, Jim. Maude's had a heart attack. She fell in the kitchen this morning."

Jack, now grown, comes out and hugs his dad. "She'll be fine," he says.

Maude hears the commotion and weakly yells, "Dearie, is that you?" Naismith strides into the bedroom and reaches for Maude's hand. The doctor checks her pulse. Hellen, now middle-aged, wipes her brow.

"Looks like I'm not going to Europe," Maude says.

Dr. Strickland quickly intervenes, "I can't recommend that. Your heart condition needs to be watched."

"I won't go either. I want to be here with you." Naismith replies.

"No! You're going. You're going for us, for our family. I'm always ruining your fun. Not this time. You're going," Maude insists as the doctor attempts to calm her down.

"Not without you."

"I have five children to watch over me. You've worked all your life for this and at 73, you're not getting any younger!" Exhausted, Maude leans back on her pillow.

"Oh, Maude. I only wish I could say with my lips what's in my heart," he cries.

"You'll be going Dr. Naismith. You'll be going. Now, tell me about New York and the plans for Denver."

Hellen, Jack, and the doctor leave. Naismith kisses Maude gently and lovingly. They cuddle and talk into the wee hours.

CHAPTER 19

THE A.A.U. FINALS

For the final game, the Refiners face their old rival, the Universals, in Denver. Pierce, avid basketball fan and movie star Boris Karloff, fellow actor John Boles, and various starlets are in the stands signing autographs. I. A. and Phog wave to the crowd, and they cheer. Ushers scurry around delivering messages and helping people to their seats.

Everything seems normal until Lubin comes out dressed as Frankenstein. The packed house screams with horror and delight. Ambitious young men take the opportunity to put an arm around their dates.

An usher approaches Pierce and says, "I'm sorry to bother you, sir." Then the usher hands him a phone message. Pierce reaches into his pocket and tips him.

"Thank you, sir," the usher says.

Pierce opens the note, scans it, and says to Karloff, "From Laemmle. Has to speak to me now."

"Go. I'll take care of things here," Karloff insists.

Pierce finds a phone booth, fumbles for the correct change, and then dials.

"Hi, June. It's Jack Pierce."

"Hold the line."

When Laemmle comes to the phone his voice is tense. "Jack—"

Pierce interrupts, "We're in the finals! It's going to be quite a game. Lubin came out as Frankenstein and got the crowd fired up—"

"Jack, I have bad news and I'll cut right to it. The bank called in our loan and they've shut down the studio. Universal Pictures is boycotting the games altogether. Remember, if you get to the Olympics, you'll have no sponsorship or corporate connection. You'll have to get to Berlin on your own."

Unfortunately, Jack already knows that the Universals are going to the Olympics. Yet, he makes every effort to help Laemmle feel better and says, "I'm sorry for your loss, sir. Maybe the team won't qualify."

"The Depression and the *Showboat* debt ruined us. The bank just wouldn't reconsider. Thank you for all you've done for the basketball team. Goodbye, Jack." Laemmle gets off the phone. It's the saddest time in his life.

"Good luck, sir." The phone clicks as Jack hangs up. He composes himself and returns to the V.I.P. section.

The Refiners look doomed. They're completely outplayed by the Universals and Carl Knowles' precision. Joe and Bill Wheatley lead the Refiners' fight. At the half, the Refiners are down by five. A Denver reporter catches up with Gene Johnson, trots with him to the dressing room, and asks, "Hey, Coach. What gives?"

"Universal just has an uncanny sense of knowing where the other fellow is going to be," Gene answers smugly and ducks into the locker room. The reporter is left without a quote and is disappointed.

At center court, Phog hurries to a just-set-up microphone, while blankets are briskly spread out on the gymnasium floor.

"Good evening and welcome to Naismith Night. I'm Phog Allen." The crowd cheers. "And I'll be brief, that's a new concept for me!" Now that he has the crowd laughing, he continues, "Dr. James Naismith has given us the game of basketball as his gift to the world. Our goal at each game is to help get Dr. Naismith to the Olympics. In these Depression times, every penny has value, and your generosity is greatly appreciated. Thank you." Phog applauds for the audience then leaves as pennies, nickels, and dimes are thrown onto the blankets. A buzzer sounds for the second half and the blankets are rolled up.

During the tip-off for the second half, Joe out jumps Lubin and the Refiners' zone defense covers the entire floor. It's a 23-6 rampage for the Refiners, and the gasping Universals are struggling to stay in the game. The Denver crowd is on its feet. Now, the Universals are down by 3. It's five minutes to go and the score is 36-33. The Universals fight back. Lubin picks up his last foul. Jack scores 6 points in an exhilarating Refiners' win, 47-35.

A Denver commentator goes to the microphone and announces, "Ladies and gentlemen, it seems that the world's tallest team is the world's best team. True champions can come from behind. Both the Refiners and the Universals move on to the Olympic Trials at Madison Square Garden. There, they'll be facing some very tough university teams."

CHAPTER 20

NO MONEY FOR THE OLYMPICS

Brundage paces in his office and chews on a cigar as phones ring in front of him. His frenetic secretary rushes in. Lyman Bingham follows her.

"Now what?" Brundage asks.

"The basketball receipts," Lyman starts.

"What about them?"

"There's no money. The plan fizzled."

"What?" Brundage's eyes pop with alarm. He can't believe what he just heard.

"We needed $200,000 to get 400 athletes to Berlin."

"And?" Brundage asks impatiently.

"We have $135,000."

"You son of a bitch! We can't fail. Why didn't you tell me sooner?" Brundage shouts.

"I didn't have all the receipts."

"How could this happen? It's that damned Hitler boycott. We've got to find that money." Brundage grabs his jacket and storms out of the office. Lyman sits shaking his head.

★   ★   ★

On final-game day, Sunday, April 5, 1936, there's a lot of commotion outside Madison Square Garden. Boycotters angrily march and protest. College team bags and equipment are misplaced on a loading dock, and there is a frenzy to get them to the players. Enterprising boys seize the moment. They grab all the bags and help carry them inside so they can get into the arena for free.

One boy says, "Come on. Follow me. We'll get to see the top college teams. You gotta' see the slam dunk."

"Okay. Let's go," agrees another boy.

The rest of the boys prepare to jump down the Garden's coal chute. "This way," he yells as he dives in head first and lands inside the huge arena. The other boys chime in, "I'm next! I'm next!" A policeman blows his whistle and the rest of the boys disperse. They wait a few minutes, then sneak back to the coal chute when the cop is gone.

Inside, the crowd ramps up for the much-publicized Refiners vs. Universals game. In the hallway, suited-up Refiners Joe and Smitty hold Coach Johnson between them. As they lift him above their heads, the reporters, including Daley, and various photographers surround them, having a field day.

Daley yells up to Gene, "Coach Johnson, the Washington Huskies just won and have been labeled the college team of 1936." Joe and Smitty gently lower Coach Johnson to the floor, and he approaches the reporters.

"We could spot any college team, including Notre Dame and Purdue, 10 to 12 points," he brags.

Daley smiles and pushes the point by asking, "What's the secret to your success?"

Gene replies, "We have a nontraditional approach. We move the ball up the floor and force the game into bad basketball and we play bad basketball better than anybody." The reporters bend over laughing as Gene makes a quick exit to the court.

The teams have warmed up. No Frankenstein. No dunks. Now they stand and wait patiently on the sidelines. As for the crowd, mania.

There are only 5,000 people in the stands and the Garden holds more than 18,000. Reporters and photographers vie for spots. Sassy groupies congregate behind the bench. Parents with kids move down to better seats, sloshing their drinks, hot dogs, and popcorn along the way.

Coach Needles pulls Coach Johnson to the side and utters, "No matter who wins this championship tonight, both our teams are going to Berlin."

Gene looks at him askance and says, "I'm the coach for the Olympics regardless."

Needles tries to be tolerant. He has no desire to placate a diva. However, he's a smart guy and knows what winning the Olympics could do for his career.

"In return for my generosity, take it easy on us tonight. All the boys need to be confident to win gold," he suggests.

"You're asking me to lose?" Gene can't believe what Needles has just asked him to do.

"No, just don't call the fire alarm. No harem-scarem or zone press. Let my team lose with dignity. Not the 18 or 20 points like you always do."

"Play 'normal' basketball."

"That would be nice."

Gene is flabbergasted and walks away, saying, "You're not a popular guy and now I see why. You're crazy if you think I'm going to tell my team to lose."

The fury is relaxed when Naismith arrives. Fans, reporters, and photographers surround him as he heads to the podium to speak. The crowd listens to every word of his opening remarks.

"It's an honor to be with you. I am humbled by your love and support. Don't be afraid to work for humanity and wait for your reward. All I ask is that you keep the game simple so that all may play. Have a good match tonight. I thank you."

After an excellent band plays a rousing version of "The Star-Spangled Banner," Gene motions the team in. They surround him. Bill takes off his warm-up pants.

"Oh, no! I didn't put on my shorts," Bill exclaims.

"Just wear your warm-ups," Jack suggests.

"I can't wear my warm-ups in the game! Give me your shorts."

Gene interjects, "Wheatley, you plan on joining us?" Coach Johnson and the team surround Bill and Jack to see what the commotion is about.

Daley notices and says to his listeners, "There seems to be some kind of controversy with the Refiners."

Back in the huddle, Bill demands, "Give me your shorts!"

"No," says Jack.

"For the team," says Bill.

"Oh, all right," Jack mumbles as he takes off his shorts. The team huddles closer around Bill and Jack as they switch outfits. Then they return to the court.

Another reporter announces, "And heeeeeere comes Bill Wheatley, the 'galloping ghost'. He just seems to appear out of nowhere."

The competition begins. Joe tips the ball. Quigley and Alvin Bell referee the game. Francis leads the fight, but the Universals' tough defense and the accurate passing of Carl Knowles and Lloyd Goldstein pokes holes in the zone defense of the Refiners.

Lubin fouls out. Sam Balter goes in.

Daley reports, "Coach Needles is subbing Sam Balter for Lubin. As a side note, the Universals' Balter and Goldstein are two Jewish boys eager to make the trip to Berlin."

The crowd cheers for them enthusiastically. It's clear that the nay-sayers are outside the arena on the picket line. Balter and Goldstein exchange a relieved and happy look, knowing that most of America is rooting for them.

In Hitler's office, there's general panic. Hitler, Goebbels, and various aides are far from relieved and happy. Goebbels hands Hitler budget paperwork to sign. Hitler is not pleased and says, "There are no budget restrictions for the Fuhrer! We're busy building concentration camps and hosting the Olympics. Just lower the laborers' pay. Say it's so all can work." Hitler hands the paperwork back to Goebbels without signing it.

Goebbels agrees, "All need to sacrifice so we can share the glory of Germany with the world. By the way, we were able to convince Helene Mayer, the Jewish fencer, to work with us on our terms, and we got Rudi Ball out of exile in France to join ice hockey." Goebbels presents the appropriate papers.

Hitler is annoyed and says, "Do we absolutely have to have those people competing with our team?"

"Yes, Fuhrer. For the Olympics only."

"Get them all out of Germany as soon as the games are over," Hitler orders as he signs the papers reluctantly.

Goebbels smiles churlishly to himself, knowing again that he has influenced the dictator, and says, "Jews will be leaving us one way or another, Fuhrer."

Back at Madison Square Garden, the final game is still under way. Brundage and Lyman survey the small crowd. The V.I.P. section is filled with Laemmle, Pierce, Karloff, Boles, and ever-present starlets. Naismith, Phog Allen, O'shaughnessy, and others represent the Refiners. The press is everywhere.

Brundage laments, "I can't believe it, five thousand people out of over 18,000 seats. This is a disgrace."

"And a thousand are from Phog Allen's new Coaches Association," Lyman informs him.

"We just better get the Olympic money or we'll look like fools," Brundage mutters as he storms out. Lyman follows, trying to figure out how he's going to fix this situation.

The game continues as the Universals' Lubin, Shy, and Knowles combine for a lethal 35 points. Francis leads an attack with 13 and fouls out. Joe lands 17.

Daley quickly reports, "The Refiners are invincible. Call it the Universals versus the 'Omnipotent' Oilers."

The Universals play up their smooth defense. Joe leaps toward the basket to swat away a Universals shot at the rim. Francis lopes by Gene and signals "harem scarem?" Gene nods "no". The team grimaces as Francis shakes his head "no" to them. Shy and Knowles take pot shots over the zone. Suddenly Joe leaps up for two points.

Daley comments, "Empire State Building Joe Fortenberry puts the win within a one-point reach: Universals 43, Refiners 42." Frantic action of several scrums and fouls ensue, and each team lands a point. The final score is 44-43. A Universals win! Laemmle, Pierce, Karloff, and their entourage cry with joy. Naismith, Phog, and others congratulate them on a game well played.

Pierce pumps Laemmle's hand and expounds, "I'm so happy for you, sir."

An ecstatic Carl Laemmle applauds with abandon and shouts, "We did it! We won! What a game!"

Daley reports, "It's over, folks. The Globe Refiners had no harem-scarem, fire, or dash left as they faced a team they've beaten many times before. For Carl Laemmle, the Olympic Trial trophy ranks right up there with an Oscar!"

The Refiners are dazed. Daley and other reporters and photographers race to Coach Needles. Daley reaches him first and blurts, "Coach Needles, congratulations. You're officially head coach of the first Olympic basketball team!"

Needles got what he wanted and graciously says, "Officially, yes, but the team will be coached by Gene Johnson. We want to incorporate all the Refiners' innovations and go for the gold!" Then Coach Needles slips into the locker room, letting Gene run the show.

With Needles gone, the reporters stampede toward Gene Johnson.

"Coach Johnson. A sad win. A loss by one point. Care to comment?" one reporter asks.

"How could I possibly be sad. The Universals and the Refiners are going to the Olympics, and we're going to win a gold medal!"

CHAPTER 21

THE INVITATION

The next day at the Brundage office, Lyman tends to a horrible cold by constantly blowing his nose. Brundage paces and remarks, "Lyman, we made only $7,000 at the Trials. Seven thousand and we needed $60,000. It's forty days until the ship sails for Berlin. How are we going to get $53,000? Figure that out."

"Cut the roster as much as possible. Then go raise the funds."

"Get the hell out of my office. I'm better off raising the money myself."

Lyman collects his Kleenex and leaves. Brundage flips on the intercom.

"Get me the police chief, then send in my next appointment, Lubin and Goldstein."

In the waiting room, Lubin and Goldstein stand and adjust their suits. Alex leads them to Brundage's office.

Brundage, all smiles, shakes hands and motions them to sit. He lets them settle, then he begins.

"Big win for the Universals, Boys! Congratulations!"

"Thank you. Thank you, sir," they reply.

"It's been brought to my attention that you have violated the most important Olympic rule: all participants must be amateurs. You two played semipro baseball."

"It wasn't Lubin, it was me. We left this big, tall fellow at home because he couldn't get away for the playoffs. It was not Lubin."

Brundage leans forward and looks directly into Lubin's eyes and asks, "Is that the story?"

Lubin looks directly back in Brundage's eyes, holds his gaze, and answers, "That's the truth."

They lock eyes and stare each other down. Brundage breaks the silence when he looks at Goldstein and declares, "So Goldstein, you're taking one for the team?"

"I'm Jewish. What am I doing in Germany?"

Brundage quickly responds, "Other countries are sending Jews."

"Sir, I'm Head Electrician at Universal Pictures. It's a dream job. I can't lose it," Goldstein flatly informs him.

"Understood," Brundage acknowledges. "I don't know how much I believe you boys, but because I don't know for sure, Lubin, we'll take you to Germany."

"Thank you, sir."

Lubin and Goldstein shake hands with Brundage and leave relieved. The phone rings. Brundage answers, "Yes, Alex."

Alex says, "Chief O'Connell is on line two."

"Put him through."

"Yes, sir."

Brundage punches line two and says, "Chief O'Connell, I hate to put you on the spot, but I need your help." He pauses then adds, "We need more cash from the police charity and we have to step up the fundraising events. We're short $53,000." He pauses to listen, then continues, "I called on you first because I know I can depend on you to get the funds fast." He deliberately pauses again, then with a big smile adds, "Thank you, Chief. Thank you in advance."

In the McPherson gym, Coach Gene Johnson watches the team execute running drills up and down the bleacher seats. Waving a telegram, he motions the team over.

"Here it is, boys, our Olympic Games invitation!" The team cheers.

Gene reads, "You are our Olympic Basketball Team. Stop. If you can get to New York by July 15, we will take you on the boat to Berlin. Stop. No corporate funds allowed, or you will be disqualified. Signed: Avery Brundage. P.S. We will contact you regarding the official fitting of the Olympic outfit."

Jack says, "We can't raise funds for all of us and the Universals? We just can't!"

Gene stops him and says, "Yes, we can. Boys, we need money for eighteen. Seven Universals, six Refiners, Needles, me, two trainers, and Phog Allen. We'll barnstorm all through America if we have to."

Meanwhile, at the basketball court on the Universal lot, Coach Needles reads the same Olympic telegram to his team that Gene Johnson just read to the Refiners.

Blonde sportsman Carl Shy grabs the telegram from Needles and responds, "What? How are we going to get that kind of money?" In the background, Sam Balter stands and leaves the group quietly.

Lubin has an idea and blurts, "We can set up exhibition dates."

Carl Knowles breaks the tense moment by saying, "Anybody have something they can sell?"

The guys confer. Needles sees that Balter is leaving and approaches him.

"Congratulations," he says. "You're the first Jew on the U.S. Olympic Team," he adds tactlessly.

Balter angrily packs his duffle bag.

"Hey, kid. Can't you take a joke?"

With angry tears, Balter says, "It's no joke, Coach. How can I compete in Berlin when every other Jew who qualified has refused?"

"It's for your team. For America," Needles reminds him.

Ballter slams on his jacket, grabs his duffle bag, and darts out, saying, "I'm done for the day. If I'm not here tomorrow, I'm not going."

Needles yells after him, "I hope we see you right here. We need you."

Back in his office, Avery Brundage toils over paperwork. Phog storms in unannounced as Alex follows him. Brundage waves her out, knowing this isn't going to be a pleasant conversation.

Angrily, Phog rants, "A 'Roving Ambassador' and pay my own way?"

"Phog, there's no money."

"No money!" I'm the one who got basketball into the Olympics!"

"You supported the Jewish boycott and I had to go to Berlin to make it right. You defended Jesse Owens' stance on race. How could you!"

"For God's sake, Avery. You're punishing me because of your own racist, anti-Semitic beliefs. The Olympics is about the best in sports, regardless of religion or race. Jesse Owens is the best. He can win gold for the United States."

"You're just sour grapes because your Jayhawkers team lost in the trials and aren't going to the Olympics. And you're supposed to be the Father of Basketball Coaching!" Phog takes a swing at Brundage and misses. Brundage grabs him and shoves him in a chair. Phog jumps out of the chair.

"I resign as Director of the American Basketball Team. I will not take the phoney, do-nothing 'Roving Ambassador' position."

Brundage tries to calm Phog down and offers, "You can self-finance and be the General Ambassador for Basketball."

"Avery, in earlier times, you might have served some good purpose. But now, you resemble a Chicago racketeer, who does not create a business or industry but steps in to tell those who did, that he is going to help run it."

Brundage storms out of his seat, "I'm not Al Capone." Then he shoves Phog out of his office.

★ ★ ★

Fortunately, the Olympians had no idea that the entire American Olympic program was in financial jeopardy. The problem was the strict donation rules stating that the Olympics could not be funded by corporations. Every aspect of the U.S. Olympics had to be amateur, including all the athletes.

The athletes' only goal was to be on the S.S. *Manhattan* Wednesday, July 15, heading for Berlin. To do that, various money-making schemes were incorporated.

On the Universal backlot, stars and extras in various costumes walk by. Pierce loads Frankenstein heads in a golf cart. Needles spots him and asks, "Can you drop me off at the gym?"

"Sure thing. Hop in."

As they drive through the lot, Needles can't help but ask, "Who really thought we'd get to go to the Olympics?" They look at each other and shake their heads.

Pierce asks, "Is Balter going?"

"Reluctantly, if they get the money. They're barnstorming … pawning their jewelry."

"I heard Lubin's doing Frankenstein guest appearances."

"He's a celebrity now. Frank, for what it's worth, I thank you and Mr. Laemmle for hiring me to coach the Universals. It's a great team."

"Just bring home the gold. Then it's completely worth it!"

They arrive at the gym and Needles says, "Coach Johnson will give it his all. I just have to do what he says!"

Pierce laughs and says, "Good luck with that!" Needles strides away from the cart chuckling and Pierce drives off.

At a haberdashery dressing room, in McPherson, Gene Johnson stands on a box before a 3-way mirror. A 5′1″ tailor finishes measuring him.

The tailor says, "Yes, I've been all over the country fitting athletes for the Olympics." He measures his arm, then says, "You have a 27-inch sleeve, sir. Voilà! You're now measured for your official wardrobe." Gene admires himself, then gets off the stand as the tailor writes his notes.

Joe enters and the tailor is stunned. He's never seen a giant before. Joe notices that if he stands on the box, his head will hit the ceiling. He moves the box to the side.

"Do you mind? I'll hit my head on the ceiling."

"No. No. Not at all."

"Thanks."

At first, the tailor starts measuring as usual, then he finds that it's easier to take the measurements by standing on the box that Joe moved to the side.

"Sleeve length, 40 inches. I have to say, I have never seen an arm that long. And I've seen a lot of arms."

Joe laughs and says, "Better get used to it. There's more on the way."

As he leaves, Smitty walks in and the tailor is shocked again.

That night, Gene and Francis set out to do some fund-raising at Uncle Lou's Barber Shop and Pool Hall. The popular establishment has bootleg whiskey in the back and gambling. Grandma Johnson tends the food counter.

The ever-silent Francis and ever-boisterous Gene are at a pool table surrounded by tipsy patrons. Francis angles his cue, eyes his opponent, stalls a bit, then hits the ball into a side pocket for the game. The winning patrons cheer. The losers pay Gene.

As he counts the money, he says, "See, it's easy to raise money for a good cause, and the Olympics is a good cause. Just like basketball. My boys love to play. The crowd loves to watch, and I love to win." The bystanders laugh and the losers walk away.

Francis sets a rack again. Another tipsy opponent steps up and Gene takes the bets. A pretty waitress serves drinks disguised in coffee mugs.

Gene continues, "Opposition doesn't like it much. I force my team to run and play hard." Francis wins another game with ease. Gene counts the additional money and says, "Then I let them win. That's the secret, I just let them win." The crowd laughs again, and Gene puts the extra cash in his pocket and says, "Let's go, Francis. We're done for now." The patrons groan as Gene and Francis leave.

CHAPTER 22

EVEN MORE PROBLEMS

At the McPherson Refinery, Joe, Smitty, Bill, Tex, Jack, and Francis are dressed up in rubber suits, boots, and hardhats. Their unglamorous entry-level job is "clean out" and they call themselves the gas plant swamp rats. If the refinery system isn't clean, then clogging will make the product impure. Sludge is the enemy, and the guys work long, hard hours in stifling heat surrounded by the boiling steam from the refinery. The goal is to get to the Olympics, and by golly, if they have to do the hottest, dirtiest job at the refinery, they will do it.

Tex says, "It'll be more sweltering heat at the gas plant today. The radio said over 100 degrees."

Jack asks, "How many extra shifts are you doing, Smitty?"

"As many as they'll let me. Straight time for 48 hours if necessary."

Jack replies, "Me, too. I'll probably die with a gauge line in my hand. You, Joe?"

Joe answers, "Count on me for whatever it takes."

Bill teases, "Let's go get 'em, you reptiles, you scorpions, you swamp rats!"

Together they yell, "Swamp rats" as they enter the refinery for a long workday.

★   ★   ★

At the same time, in a Universal make-up trailer, Boris Karloff puts down his newspaper and admires his haircut. John Boles waits for a shave by reading the *The Wall Street Journal*. Jack Pierce barges in and says, "Boris, I need your help." Boris waves out the barber. When he leaves, Karloff asks, "How's the basketball funding?"

"Terrible. We don't have the money," Pierce answers.

"It would be pathetic if the team didn't go to the Olympics," Boles laments.

Pierce is desperate and wants to know just where Karloff stands, and asks, "Boris, can you get the money?"

"How much?"

"The boys have raised $500. So, $2,000."

Karloff doesn't skip a beat and says, "I'll put in $1500. John, you in for $500?"

John quickly opens his briefcase, finds his checkbook, and starts writing.

"Here's the check right now," Boles answers assertively.

"Thank you, gentlemen. I'll get the train tickets today," Pierce says as he rushes out the door relieved that his team will make it to New York.

★　★　★

In the refinery locker room, the tired team members peel off their filthy work clothes and one by one head into the showers.

"With all our double shifts, it looks like we have the money. Let's go celebrate," Bill suggests.

"Good idea," Smitty says as he lumbers to the shower.

Joe asks, "Bill, how's the German class going?"

Jack teases, "Can you say 'Heil Hitler'?" Bill snaps his towel at Jack as they head for the showers.

"Would you stop bugging me? If I'm going to Germany, I just think it's a good idea to speak German," Bill answers logically.

In the shower, Smitty turns on the warm, welcoming water. When he steps back to enjoy the warmth, he slices his heel on a piece of tin stripping. Thinking it's minor, he calmly looks down and watches his blood spew. Horrified, he yells, "Ah, shit! Hey, Joe. Come here!" Joe gets up, goes to the shower, sees the blood and grabs a towel to stop the bleeding.

"Geez! Somebody call the doctor!"

Jack, dripping wet, rushes to the phone and says, "S.O.S. We have a man down in the locker room." Then he joins the rest of the team surrounding Smitty as he hobbles to a bench.

For safety reasons, a refinery doctor is on call for every shift. He is prepared for emergencies and can treat anything and everything, especially heatstroke and burns. The doctor arrives promptly and examines Smitty's foot.

He says, "Get to my office. You need stitches."

Smitty speedily rewraps his foot in the towel and the team makes a human chair. Quickly, they rush him down the hall.

In the doctor's office, Smitty and the doctor are surrounded by the team.

"We leave for New York in two weeks," says Joe.

The doctor responds, "Don't worry. He'll make it."

Smitty pledges, "Nothing's keeping me away from Berlin! Anyway, I play on my toes. Who needs a heel?" The team guffaws and the doctor starts stitching.

Now the time seems to move entirely too slowly, like waiting for water to boil. Both teams try to stay relaxed as they prepare to leave for Berlin.

On July 3, a bored Joe and Tex sit at McPherson's Echo Café counter. Abe spots them and asks, "What can I get for you boys?"

Joe answers, "I'll have a large water and some of your special coffee."

"Make that two special coffees," adds Tex.

Abe serves them. They take their drinks and move to a booth. Two men, Ed and Bob stop by to say hello.

"Hi, I'm Ed. I own the local Chevy dealership, and this here is Bob, my top associate. We'd sure love to take you boys out for a drive to celebrate the Fourth."

"No thanks," Joe replies. "We have to get ready for the Olympics. Pack and all."

"In five days we leave for New York to board the *S.S. Manhattan* going to Berlin," Tex mentions.

Bob says, "The breeze will sure feel good, and we have some moonshine on ice to share with you."

Again, Joe says, "No thanks," and takes a sip of his coffee.

Ed senses that Joe and Tex can still be convinced so he adds, "Not to mention some fun girls to help celebrate America's birthday." Joe and Tex exchange a look.

"Actually, a party sounds great," Tex agrees. Joe smiles and says to Tex, "Really?" Then Joe shrugs and says, "Okay. What can it hurt? Anything to get cool."

Ed extends his hand to shake and says, "Terrific! We'll see you right here tomorrow at noon."

★   ★   ★

Bob was right: the breeze is wonderful on this sweltering, hot day. Ed speeds along the highway with Bob, Joe, Tex, and two pretty girls in a red 1936 Chevy convertible. It has a white interior with red piping, and the radio is booming. They speed past sunflower farms and cattle ranches, and drink moonshine as they hoot it up.

As Ed picks up speed, Bob begins to get nervous and fidgety. He says to Ed, "Hey, slow down. Precious cargo."

"We gotta' get around this truck and really let her rip," Ed says. He swerves and tries to pass a semi-truck in front of him. No luck, so he slows down a bit.

Joe leans out the side and sees cars coming from a distance, then says, "That's okay. You don't have to pass. We got it."

Tex picks up on what Joe is saying and adds, "Let's head back."

Ed guns the motor and veers into the shoulder to try to pass. Everyone in the car grabs something to hold on to.

Joe says, "Holy shit!"

Tex says," Jesus!"

Bob screams, "Are you nuts?!"

The car slides on the gravel and rolls and rolls down a hill then, finally stops. Ed, Bob, and the girls scramble out of the car to look to see if anyone is hurt. They see Tex lying on the grass, limp and bleeding. He might be dead. They rush to him, surround him, and start shaking his body. Finally, he moves and groans. The girls tend to Tex, while Ed and Bob look for Joe.

Joe has rolled further down the hill into some brush. He staggers to his feet and lurches toward the car. When he sees Tex, Joe takes off his jacket and wraps it around Tex's bleeding arm.

Angrily, Joe says, "This ride's over. Get us to a hospital."

Ed, Bob, and girls run to the road to flag down a car.

Tex wonders aloud and says to Joe, "Can anything else go wrong?"

"With only four days until we leave for New York, it better not," Joe answers.

In the Naismith living room, Maude rests quietly in her easy chair and reads the mail to Naismith as he straightens his tie and checks his luggage. The doorbell rings.

"That's John," Naismith says as he dashes for the door.

Maude reads aloud, "By gosh, Phog kept his word. It says here that he got $2,771.57 from 43 states. John mowed lawns for you. The bake sales were a success!"

"It won't be the same without you."

Maude says, "I'll be honeymooning with you every step of the way."

Naismith opens the door and says, "John, come in. Thank you for mowing the lawn today. How much do I owe you?"

"Absolutely nothing. In fact, I want you to have this." John pulls out his prized 50-cent piece and puts it in Naismith's hand.

"Oh, John. This means too much to you. I can't take it," Naismith pleads as he tries to give the coin back to John.

"Yes, you can," John says as he folds the coin back into Naismith's hand. "It's for good luck. I'll be rooting for you, sir."

"Thank you, John. Thank you so much. I'll keep it in my pocket all through the Olympics."

They backslap and John quickly exits with Naismith's luggage.

Naismith returns to Maude. She hugs him, then says, "Go, Dearie. You have a wonderful time in Germany and kiss all the relatives in Scotland for me."

"I'll write every day."

"I can't wait for you to get back and tell me all about it."

They lovingly kiss and Naismith leaves.

★   ★   ★

At the Universal Studios telegraph office, a foxy assistant files messages. Lubin ducks in the doorway.

She asks, "Can I help you?"

"I need to send a telegram. It's to my dad and mom in New York."

The assistant seductively gets her pad to jot down the wording and says, "Okay."

Lubin finds his notes and says, "Don't get on the boat to go to Berlin until you see us there."

"That bad?" the assistant asks.

"We got the money. Now we have to get to the ship on time. Nothing can go wrong." He pays her and as he leaves, she says, "Come back soon."

★   ★   ★

In New York, the women's track team won't let something like no money stop them from going to the Olympics. They sell Olympic badges on the street in all five New York boroughs. When they arrive, crowds immediately surround the star athletes to buy the badges and to wear them with pride.

"Here's a badge. That'll be a dollar," says one pretty team member as she takes the dollar and hands a badge to an eager little girl. "Thank you," she adds. The child skips away happily. She turns and a Harlem boy approaches her and pulls out ten 3-cent stamps from his pocket and gives them to her.

She says, "I shouldn't take your only stamps."

"Yes, you should," he argues. "I want Jesse Owens to run in the Olympics. I think he can win a gold medal."

"I think he can win, too."

She takes the stamps and gives the kid a hug and a badge. He runs off ecstatic.

CHAPTER 23

ON THE WAY TO BERLIN

At Union Station in Los Angeles, families, friends, and fans send off Needles and the seven Universal basketball players with festive banners and U.S.A. flags.

A lady in the crowd yells, "Bring back the gold."

Some teens join in with, "Root for Jesse! Root for Jesse!"

The men board the train thrilled and excited. Now they just have to get to New York on time. Joyously, the players and Needles wave to their fans as they depart. The train chugs out of the station and speeds through the Rockies and the plains. Along the way, the men see things they've never seen before, such as moose and bison. They stare out the windows of the fleeting train at America, the beautiful.

In the McPherson gym parking lot, the local high school band plays as banners flap in the breeze. Two sedans, loaded with rope-tied luggage, glisten in the heat. Townsfolk, including families, cute girls, Grandma Johnson, Phog, John McLendon, and Abe, stuff the autos with sack lunches, bags of fruit, and bottles of soda for the six-day trek. The team gathers near the cars, and the crowd surrounds them.

Gene stands beside his car and shouts to the crowd, "We're on our way! Twelve hundred miles to New York City. We've got two cars, one coach, six basketball players, and thanks to your generos-ity, extra shifts, and pool hustling, enough cash to make it."

There are loud cheers from the crowd and they chant, "U.S.A. U.S.A. U.S.A."

Gene hops into the driver's seat of the first car. Tex, with his arm and head bandaged, sits behind him. Smitty sits next to Tex with his wrapped foot stretched out and balanced on the folded-down front seat.

"Oh, great! I get the infirmary," Gene quips.

"Then I know you'll drive safely," Francis yells from the other sedan.

Francis starts his engine. Joe, Jack, and Bill pile in: Jack shot-gun, Bill behind Francis, and Joe behind Jack. Finally, they're off to New York.

They wave good-bye to what seems like the entire town of McPherson as the crowd blows kisses and cheers. When the crowd is out of sight, Bill loosens his tie and sits as comfortably as possible with his books in the corner. Jack is eager, ready to navigate, and watches the road intently. Joe arranges their jackets neatly in the window tray behind him and does his best to settle in.

Jack casually opens one of the bags and says, "Food! We gotta' make it last. I only have $25."

Bill asks, "How do you expect to go to Germany and home on $25?"

"I may starve, but I'm going to the Olympics! Who needs to eat?"

Joe rolls his eyes and stretches out as leisurely as possible with a leg outside Jack Ragland's window.

"We'll share," Joe suggests.

Francis assures them, "Hey guys, relax. We have plenty of money. We're covered." With that, Bill starts to read. Joe and Jack try to nap while Francis happily drives.

Wheat fields seem to gently wave good-bye, and sunflower farms seem extra cheery as the cars whiz by. It's as if all of Kansas is wishing them luck. Passing the LEAVING MCPHERSON, POP. 6147 sign is like a period at the end of a sentence. Their lives will never be the same.

In his office, Avery Brundage puffs on his ever-present cigar. Lyman is there, surrounded by accounting paperwork, an adding machine, and his Kleenex.

Brundage rants, "Dammit. It's July 10. I have boys driving across America. Athletes on trains coming from the West. Everybody is on the way. How am I going to tell them I'm still $11,000 short, can't make the last payment on the ship fare, and they aren't going to Berlin? The conflict-of-interest rules are ruining us."

Lyman optimistically says, "We have yet to hear from the police department's charity drive. That will include the ladies' track and field, and swim events, and their badge sales. Sergeant O'Connell will be here soon."

"This is a disaster. My career is over," Brundage mumbles as he paces.

Meanwhile, the two sedans speed through America, past the Mississippi river and the Appalachians, toward Manhattan's mesmerizing skyline. At last, they see the WELCOME TO NEW YORK CITY sign that boasts Pop. 6,930,446. They sit up with reverence and admire the hustle-bustle of New Yorkers. Near the same time, the Universals' Sky Chief zooms toward Manhattan. The men are playing cards, reading, and napping.

Back at the Brundage office, Brundage is still waiting. He alternates between pacing and sitting, pacing and sitting. Then he lights up another cigar. Lyman does his best to look busy as he slyly checks his watch.

Brundage asks, "Is it 4 yet?"

"3:56. Sergeant's never late," Lyman responds.

The phone rings and Brundage lunges for it. Alex asks if they would like sandwiches.

"No, no sandwiches. Thank you, Alex."

Brundage hangs up impatiently and resumes his pacing. Soon, the phone rings again. This time he lets it ring. Lyman calmly leans over and answers it. Alex informs him that Sergeant O'Connell is here.

Lyman says, "Send him in."

Sergeant O'Connell is a good-looking, middle-aged man who takes great pride in his work. He serves as head of the N.Y.P.D. Police Academy and confidently strides in with a huge smile.

"Please tell me some good news," Brundage begs.

O'Connell dips into his pocket, pulls out a folded check, hands it to Brundage, and says, "I hope this helps."

Brundage takes a moment, then opens the check. He reads it and exclaims, "$12,384.56. He jumps up from his chair and hugs Sergeant O'Connell. I love your charity and I love your charity ladies. Thank you!" He looks up toward the heavens and adds, "America, we're on our way to the Olympics!"

In the Francis Johnson car, morale is at a low. Clearly the men are tired and weary, and have had too much time to think. As Francis drives, he says, "Bill, I know you've been studying for months, but don't speak German in Germany. It might not be safe. They might think you're Jewish."

Bill replies, "Nobody will notice. But I get the point." With a sigh, Bill closes his German book, methodically grabs the other German study materials, and tosses them out the window.

He says, "I don't want any trouble. The only thing important is to win the gold."

In Gene Johnson's car, the group is more restless. Tex pulls out a pair of scissors and nods to Smitty.

Tex asks Smitty, "Ready?"

Smitty gets out his scissors and answers, "Ready. I've waited long enough."

They start cutting their bandages carefully.

Gene heatedly asks, "Hey! What are you boys doing?"

"We're not showing up in New York looking injured," Smitty answers. Then he adds, "I'm walking into that fancy hotel looking like a winner."

Tex chimes in, "Like champions. Like nothing ever happened."

At the Hotel Lincoln, the sweaty Refiners haul their sparse luggage into the luxury building's lobby. It was named for Abraham Lincoln and it's the newest and largest hotel in New York City, claiming 27 stories and 1,331 rooms. Located at 700 Eighth Avenue, between 44 and 45 Streets, it houses the famous Blue Room restaurant and is a popular gathering spot for the elite.

As they check-in, the tired Universal team arrives. They greet each other warmly, relieved that the whole team made it in time. Exhausted, they all leave for their rooms.

Joe, Smitty, and Lubin board the elevator together. When they reach their floor, Joe says to Lubin, "See you tomorrow at the ship."

"See you there," he replies.

Joe and Smitty head toward their room.

In the hotel room, Joe and Smitty can't help but stare at all the luxury. Yep, it's fancy. The two put down their luggage and look around. They sit on the twin beds that have matching silk bedspreads and then stretch out. Much, much better than the car! Very comfy.

They get up and turn on the water in the sink and in the shower: hot and cold, nifty. Then there are the fluffy towels and the customized little soaps. This is opulent living and they'll take it!

When they start unpacking, Joe opens the closet door and stops in his tracks. Smitty notices Joe is staring at something and he goes to him to check it out. He stops in his tracks as well. There it is. The show stopper:

Hanging in the closet are the official Olympic outfits: navy blazer with the U.S.A. emblem; white pants; white straw hat; shirts; red, white, and blue striped neckties; shoes; and even socks. With tears in their eyes, Joe and Smitty touch the garments and take a moment to let it all sink in.

CHAPTER 24

THE *S.S. MANHATTAN*

On July 15, 1936, the *S.S. Manhattan* is nestled in her berth at Pier 60. It's 10:30 a.m. and already 100 degrees. The magnificent ship is dazzling white with a bright red hull. American flags adorn the railing and flap in the hot breeze.

At the dock, a New York band plays. Seven thousand people eagerly wait to send off the boat. Among them is Phog Allen. The crowd yells and cheers as the athletes and V.I.P.s arrive.

The media are everywhere. Newsreel crews film and flashbulbs pop. The crowd goes wild when movie sensations Boris Karloff, John Boles, and Eleanor Holm arrive. Eleanor leads the swim team with all the flare of a superstar. After all, she was Jane in *Tarzan* and won a gold medal in the 1932 Olympics in the 100-meter backstroke.

Now she sports a revealing low-cut dress complete with a white fur stole in the hottest summer on record. Eleanor's own photographer and newsreel crew scamper by her side. She is escorted by her band leader husband, Art Jarrett, and his band members.

At the top of the gangplank, Brundage shakes each guest's and athlete's hand, and Van Ritter gives each a small American flag.

Boarding is swimmer Alfred Joaquin, who has been chosen to carry the U.S. flag at the opening ceremony. His teammate Wally O'Connor joins him. Then the rowing team arrives with 5'4" cockswain Bobby Moch. Next, the running team receives huge cheers for Jesse Owens, Ralph Metcalfe, and Mathew "Mack" Robinson. Mack is baseball great Jackie Robinson's older brother by four years. He will come in second to Jesse Owens and win the silver medal. Archie Williams, John Woodruff, Marty Glickman, and Sam Stoller join them. Brundage, in his best I'm-not-racist demeanor, shakes the ever-gracious Jesse's hand and makes sure the camera gets a shot.

Others to arrive are *The New York Times* reporter Arthur Daley and other members of the press. Randolph Hearst and his movie-star wife, Marion Davies, mingle among them. Then, the basketball team arrives. Their height is so noticeable that the best thing they can do is to try to be normal. Brundage stares up at Joe, Smitty, and Lubin in amazement. By this time, the team is used to being stared at, and they handle it with a graciousness beyond the call of duty.

As the Goodyear blimp circles overhead and planes fly in formation, the ship horn bellows. Black smoke billows from the funnels, and tugs gracefully turn the ship out to sea.

Elated athletes wave their miniature American flags. It's quite a site. The band on the shore plays. The crowd cheers and waves. Phog Allen looks on with tears of happiness in his eyes. His mission is complete. Basketball is in the Olympics, and the team is determined to bring home the gold.

In the distance, the zeppelin *Hindenburg*, with its massive swastikas on the fin, leads the way to Germany. As the *S.S. Manhattan* passes the Statue of Liberty, the athletes put their hands over their hearts. Unified as one, the 1936 U.S. Olympic Team is on its way to win.

Out in the ocean and with the fanfare over, it's a mad dash to settle into the rooms. Joe and Lubin notice the rowing crew struggle, trying to secure their boat on a high rafter. Bobby Moch is standing on storage boxes, directing a member of the rowing team, Don Hume.

Joe says, "You boys need some help?"

Bobby stops directing and stares up at Joe with his jaw dropped. Then he turns his gaze toward Lubin, saying, "Yeah. We could use some." With a move as graceful as a basketball pass, Joe and Lubin easily secure the boat and head to their rooms.

Hume asks, "What was that?"

Bobby answers, "I think it was the basketball team." Then he yells down the hall, "Thank you!" but Joe and Lubin are long gone.

In the main dining room, a welcome luncheon is in full swing. The buffet is gorgeous and abounding with a variety of quality food. There are carving stations for beef, turkey, and ham. Salads, soups, and practically any vegetable an athlete could want are there for the taking. Many make a straight line for the desserts first, since you could have as many as you wanted. But the open-air bar at the side of the dining hall is the place with the most action.

Brundage steps center stage to the microphone and says, "I want to officially welcome each of you. You're the best of the best in all America. Now we have eight days together on the beautiful high seas." The athletes applaud.

"A few rules," Brundage continues. "No overeating and specifically no over*drinking*. Remember your purpose and that you are representing America." He holds out his glass to toast, "Now have a good time and go for the gold!" Brundage toasts and they all drink up. Al Jarrett strikes up the live music and dancing begins. The party gets wilder and wilder. There's no racism or separatism of any kind. They party all night and have a blast!

Meanwhile, on the Berlin streets, there's a frantic drive to complete the preparations for the Olympics. Urgently, the Gestapo shoots guns in the air to root out Gypsies. They burn their tents and load them on military trucks.

"Get on the damned truck, you heathens," a gestapo officer barks. "No Jews or Gypsies on the streets during the Olympics."

A Gypsy child frantically looks for her mother. The mother has been wounded. A cruel Gestapo officer grabs the mother and puts her on one truck. "Wounded go here," he says. When he sees the screaming child, he puts her on another truck, yelling, "Now, I'll give you something to cry about. You'll never see your mother again."

At a Berlin news station, papers with anti-Semitic caricatures are quickly taken off the stands. Prostitutes and gays are rounded up and arrested.

In the Olympic stadium, beautiful, smart filmmaker Leni Riefenstahl and her crew dig holes, lay dolly track, and determine the highest camera angles for the epic movie *Olympiad*. No expense has been spared. Hitler is to seem like a god on the movie screen, and Leni has the skills to make him the star he craves to be worldwide.

A few days later, on the *S.S. Manhattan*, decks are full of bored athletes working out in windy conditions. Some get seasick and throw up into the ocean. Basketballers Balter and Bishop practice ping-pong. Divers plunge into the ocean with rope around their waists and are brought to the surface like fish. Runners jog in and out of deck chairs. Some athletes play cards and read. Joe and Lubin pass a basketball to and fro. Suddenly, a wave comes along and knocks the basketball toward the railing. Quickly, they dive for it, but to no avail as the ball sails into the ocean. Joe and Lubin look at each other sadly.

"That's our last ball," Joe says. "I guess we could go to the variety show again."

"Not much variety," Lubin replies.

"To the bar?" Joe suggests.

"Nothing else to do."

Joe and Lubin ease toward the bar and see the team. They amuse themselves with eating and drinking contests and autograph hopping.

On the Berlin streets, a final clean-up is in progress of the picturesque Germany Hitler wants the world to see. Decorators busily bring in colorful plants and hang red swastika banners and flags.

The *S.S. Manhattan* finally arrives at its berth in Berlin. Excited Olympic athletes hurry to one side of the ship for the first view of Germany. Smiling Germans wave miniature Olympic flags. The worldwide press, with their cameras, microphones, and other equipment, pack the surroundings.

Daley reports, "The event of the century, folks. Germany is expecting 4,500 athletes from 52 countries, and 105 news people will broadcast to 40 nations."

As teams disembark, the city goes wild. Teens compete to touch the shoulders of the basketball players. Some people carry small scissors and try to snip souvenirs of cloth or hair from the athletes, especially Jesse Owens. The athletes run toward the awaiting busses for safety.

On his office balcony, Hitler sits and enjoys a cigarette while he admires the view of marching Hitler Youth. It brings him great joy and hope when he sees the excellent way the youth are being prepared. A *Der Sturmer* newspaper with a hideous Jewish caricature rests on his lap.

Goebbels enters and says, "All the athletes have arrived, Fuhrer."

Hitler motions for him to sit. Goebbels finds a chair next to Hitler, reaches for a cigarette, and lights up. They sit in silence for a few moments, enjoying their cigarettes and the beautiful day.

Then Hitler says, "Our people will be more charming than the Parisians, more easygoing than the Viennese, more vivacious than the Romans, more cosmopolitan than London, and more practical than New York."

"It's Germany's destiny," Goebbels replies.

They continue to watch the Hitler Youth march and smoke in silence. Each is in his own thoughts about the dream he has for himself and for Germany.

CHAPTER 25

THE OLYMPIC VILLAGE

At the German dock, it seems like organized bedlam. Athletes from all over the world hop onto assigned swastika-adorned busses. The Canadian basketball team (Jim Stewart with his wife; Ian Allison; Gordon Aitchison; Art and Chuck Chapman, lugging their video camera; Edward Dawson; Irving Meretzky; heartthrob Doug Peden; Malcolm Wiseman; Stanley Nantais; and Coach "Gordy" Fuller) disembarks from their ship just as the American team disembarks from the *S.S. Manhattan*. They see each other for the first time and, in silence, size each other up.

The Americans have heard about "pretty boy" Peden, Canada's top basketball scorer. The Canadians can't help but gawk at the tall American team—intimidating to say the least—but the Canadian team keeps its composure as there are many distractions. Military units drill openly, Hitler Youth march, and gliders swoop over the tourists to impress.

Bill, Joe, and the rest of the team climb onto their bus, which has its own Gestapo chaperone. The running team joins them. Black athletes head to the back of the bus by habit. All notice these aren't just busses. Joe nearly hits his head on a protruding object.

Joe asks Bill, "Is this a gun mount?"

"Sure looks like it," Bill answers.

The basketball team, including Balter, and the running team, with Jesse Owens, Robinson, Howe, Metcalfe, Glickman, and Stoller, settle into their seats and stare out the windows of the bus. Cobblestone streets are bedecked with Olympic banners and flags. Uniformed street cleaners dispose of any animal droppings. Waving, smiling, happy Germans throw flowers and rose petals toward the Olympians' busses as they pass. The team happily smiles and waves back. As the bus pulls away, there are visible undercarriages showing that it's possible for the bus to be converted into a tank.

Since the Olympic Village is isolated from Berlin, Germany has made sure there's plenty to see along the way. There are the picturesque streets with planes flying in formation over them. The *Hindenburg* hovers. Nazis surround the village with their guns visible as Olympic flags flap above them. It's obvious every detail has been directed and choreographed.

Three adorable German boys, ages 8, 10, and 12, and a Gestapo chaperone board the bus. The boys wear Hitler Youth uniforms with a special shirt. Hans, the eight-year-old has a lisp, which adds to his cuteness.

Hans reads from his handwritten paper, "Welcome, Americans, to your home for three weeks. We are happy to have you in Germany. Heil Hitler!"

The boys salute and the Gestapo chaperone beams with pride. The bus moves toward the village as the boys point out the sites.

Twelve-year-old Ernst speaks flawless English. He's very proud and a bit arrogant. He adds, "It is our honor to be your guides. We have worked hard to be able to interpret for you."

"In fact, we all had to make straight As," jokes fun-loving Fritz, the 10-year-old. Everybody loves Fritz and the whole bus is full of joy.

Ernst quickly restores order. "Please ask any boy you see in this uniform for directions."

"Or if you need anything," Hans adds.

As they turn into the Olympic Village, a charming, undulating patchwork of birch forests, lakes, clearings, cottages, and exotic animals, the team can't help but be in awe. Athletes from other countries swim in the lakes and bask in chaise lounges. The camaraderie is infectious. The team can't wait to get off the bus, unpack, and settle in.

Fritz continues, "There are 140 cottages, a shopping mall with a barber shop and sauna." The team watches as other athletes go in and out of various stores.

Hans says, "A Post Office. A dentist. A hospital. Training facilities and busses to take you anywhere you want to go any time."

"The busses are coordinated for the schedule of events," Ernst adds.

"Each country has a dining hall with its own chefs and specifications. Americans get ice cream," Hans exclaims.

Ernst says, "You can savor native or any of the 37 other dining halls. Most exciting is our advanced technology. Take a moment to go to the main office and see 'television' on exhibit. They say it's like a radio combined with a little movie screen."

Clearly, the Americans are impressed. When the bus comes to a stop, the Gestapo chaperone rises from his seat to applaud the boys as they disembark. The teams applaud as well. When the doors are closed, the Gestapo announces, "And Aryan gentlemen, for your personal pleasure—" Owens, Robinson, Metcalfe, Balter, Glickman and Stoller look away.

The Gestapo continues with pride, "We have the very discreet Love Garden. We're providing free sexual attention from our prettiest, health-approved maidens 24 hours a day."

The men are stunned. Gene Johnson looks at the basketball team, nodding "no."

As if on cue, the bus stops at the basketball cottage and the men unload. In their new home, the men start to unpack and spot dark curtains neatly rolled up over the windows and door.

Art looks a little closer and asks the guys, "Are these camouflage hooks?"

Lubin joins him and asks, "And blackout curtains?"

The guys stop unpacking to look. Lubin heads toward Balter protectively and adds, "They've figured out all the possibilities. You know, if Berlin were to get bombed."

Joe picks up on Lubin's protectiveness toward Balter and says, "Let's win gold and get the hell out of here."

CHAPTER 26

THE UNBELIEVABLE NEW RULES

Meanwhile, coaches Gene Johnson and Jimmy Needles don't even unpack. They immediately seek out where the basketball games are going to be played and head out to take a tour of the courts. They quickly find that they can't go anywhere unattended. They are accompanied by a Gestapo chaperone and a German International Olympic Committee (I.O.C.) official everywhere they go. When the coaches see the outdoor basketball courts, they are shocked to say the least.

Gene, trying to not lose his temper, mentions, "These are clay courts."

The official beams with pride and says, "Yes. The finest open-air space available. We have combined sand, clay, and minerals to make the hardest court possible. The markings are of the best ground chalk, and the ball has been specially designed by Berg." The Official uncovers a ball and presents it to Gene.

Gene is dumbfounded but still tries to remain calm and says, "There must be some mistake. This is not a basketball."

Needles adds testily, "And this is not a basketball court."

"Ah, yes. It's our very finest," the official reminds him.

Gene storms off with the ball toward the Olympic athletic office. Needles follows. The official and the chaperone hurry after them.

At the basketball office, Brundage and German I.O.C. officials huddle with Swiss and Estonian referees.

Gene barges in and yells, "You're forcing all the teams to use untanned leather balls?" Gene throws the ball to Needles and it waffles to the side.

Needles catches the ball and, enraged, adds, "The raised stitching makes the ball lopsided."

"It's smooth, with no grains like a balloon ball," Gene says.

Needles readies himself to throw the ball back to Gene and says, "Watch, the wind catches it. You can't grab it." Needles throws the ball to Gene and he misses.

Gene says, "See, it can't be thrown straight. It's too light. There's no accuracy, even from an easy pass." Then Gene tries to dribble.

"And this ball won't dribble."

Quickly an official interjects, "Dribbling is against the rules."

Now Gene is livid and forces himself into the official's face and yells, "What?"

Needles grabs Gene and pulls him away and asks the official, "What are the rules? Could we see the rules, please?"

The Estonian referee reads aloud, "No 'flying'." Then he says, "I think you call it 'traveling'. Foot movement is a foul."

Needles tries to make sense of this and says, "So, no dribbling."

"Little or no contact," the Estonian referee declares.

Gene has calmed down and inquires, "Why weren't we given these rules in advance? A clay court. No dribbling. Clearly un-American and un-Canadian rules!"

"Dusty clay, brick dust, and sweat equals slick," Needles concludes aloud.

The Estonian referee continues reading, "Only seven men can suit up per game."

Gene throws up his arms in disgust and leaves, slamming the door. Needles follows.

The ever-diplomatic Brundage steps forward and says, "For some reason, they just haven't been exposed to the rules. I assure you, they will be fine." Brundage leaves as the others continue reading the rules.

Gene and Needles join the team on the converted tennis court. They don't enjoy knowing that they have some serious decisions to make. When they see the team searching for a rhythm and trying to figure out how to use the ball on the clay surface, it all seems lost.

Gene forges on and says to Needles, "We brought fourteen men and we're playing them all."

"Absolutely," Needles agrees.

"We'll divide them up, basically into the Universal Sure Passers and the Refiner Wild Men."

"And for the last game—" Needles inquires.

"Whatever strategy will work," Gene says.

They look up when they hear the Canadian basketball team confidently jog by, led by the dashing Doug Peden.

Needles points and says, "That's the team to beat. They're athletic and husky. Doug Peden is the one to stop."

Gene says, "I'm more worried about Mexico. They're fast and cagey and full of surprises. I don't like surprises."

Brundage arrives in his car, spots the tennis courts, and then Gene. He strides up to him and asks, "Coach, could I have a word with you?"

Gene nods to Brundage and Needles takes over. Needles blows his whistle and starts a passing drill. Gene meets with Brundage on the side of the court.

"Yes, Mr. Brundage, what's the verdict?" Gene asks.

Brundage leans into Coach Johnson and says in a very civil voice, "If you ever embarrass me again in front of the International Olympic Committee, I will have you and the entire American basketball team suspended from the games."

The coach knows he's trapped because Brundage has the power and the cruelty to act on his threat. Gene says, "The rules are stacked against us. The rules favor the Europeans—"

Brundage interrupts, "who play the game outdoors and have the right to set rules for everyone."

"It's just not—"

Brundage interrupts again "I don't want this to be difficult, Coach. Please don't make me do something you will regret." As Brundage signals for his car, a shaken and humiliated Gene turns his back on Brundage and walks toward the team. Brundage steps inside the car and is driven off.

Gene watches the team as they practice. They work together to get used to the new rules, but there are many, many mistakes. Gene huddles with the boys.

Gene says, "We have one week to figure this out. Our practice time is in the afternoon. Go to any events you want in the morning. But be back early for practice. We have a lot of work to do."

CHAPTER 27

THE OPENING CEREMONY

Finally, it's the Opening Ceremony at the Olympic stadium. Each athlete is proudly wearing the uniform of their country. Americans wear their white flannel pants (skirts for the women); navy blazers; red, white, and blue striped ties; and white straw hats. Each American athlete's credentials are verified at the gate to make sure they match the list held by a Gestapo officer. The basketball team is passed through. Naismith and Gene Johnson are next. Naismith hands the Gestapo officer his badge and paperwork.

The very discerning Gestapo officer hands Naismith back his badge and paperwork and says, "You're not on the list." Then he turns to the next person in line and orders, "Next."

"What?" Gene asks as he tries to look on the list. "He invented basketball. One of the Olympic sports." The Gestapo officer pulls his list away so Gene can't see it and adds huffily, "he's not on the list."

Naismith inquires, "Would you kindly look again?"

Impatiently, the Gestapo looks again and says, "You're not on the list."

"That's impossible," Naismith says.

"You will have to see Mr. Brundage," the Gestapo informs them as he points to Brundage in the background. Livid, Gene charges toward Brundage and angrily says, "What do you think you're doing?"

"Making sure you do as I say," Brundage replies coldly. Gene hauls off to slug Brundage. Naismith stops him.

Brundage glares at Gene and says, "I think I've made my point."

Then Brundage motions for his car and leaves. Naismith and Gene are left outside the arena and don't see the Opening Ceremony.

Gene says, "I'm so sorry, Dr. Naismith. This all my fault."

Naismith comforts him and says, "No, it's politics. Just go out there and win. Win the gold for America."

The *Hindenburg* lolls above the stadium, which has the colorful flags from each nation around its parapet. Leni Riefenstahl films as 110,000 people cheer when a blonde torch bearer enters the stadium. He races toward a huge bronze caldron nestled on a tripod.

At exactly 3:58 p.m., an enormous bell tolls, composer Richard Strauss conducts *Deutschland*, and Hitler, impeccably dressed, arrives in his Mercedes convertible. The crowd, including thousands of youth, extend their arms to salute and shout in unison, "Sieg Heil! Sieg Heil! Sieg Heil!"

Hitler takes his position on the podium. He looks and acts like a king surrounded by loyal subjects. The slightly cloudy sky seems to open up as if welcoming his ascension. His eyes glisten. A five-year-old girl gives him a delicate bouquet of white flowers. He beams. The cameras roll for the first and spectacular March of Nations. All countries, starting with Greece, enter one by one and dip their flags as they pass Hitler.

The U.S.A. athletes sing *The Gang's All Here* as they adjust their straw hats and get into an eight-abreast formation. In the dark cement tunnel to the stadium, the shuffling sound of their footsteps is drowned out by the cheering for the countries before them. Upon their entering the stadium, the orchestra plays, the crowd cheers, and the sun bursts through the clouds, making this seem like a religious awakening. It all adds up to an inspiring moment as the United States makes its entrance.

The Americans are amazed at the grandeur. Alfred Joachim carries the flag as high as he can. Taller water polo player Wally O'Connor grabs the flag and raises it higher as the U.S. passes Hitler. The Americans do not "Heil Hitler." They place their hats over their hearts and gaze at the Stars and Stripes as they march. Hitler unhappily shifts in his seat. Goebbels glares at the obvious disrespect. Dignitaries frown. The crowd applauds politely, while stamping their feet, adding catcalls and boos.

When the crowd settles, Strauss strikes an opening fanfare that causes all 110,000 people to jump to their feet. As host nation, Germany enters last in crisp white linen suits and white yachting caps. The crowd extends their right arms and shouts, "Sieg Heil! Sieg Heil! Sieg Heil!" The German athletes are in perfect formation and in perfect step as their national anthem is played. The Americans see this and they deliberately walk out of step.

When the German athletes finish their entrance, attention is quickly directed to the welcoming microphone as Theodor Lewald, President of the German Olympic Committee, offers gratitude to Hitler and the German people.

Finally, he wraps it up and says, "And now, our Fuhrer, Sieg Heil!"

The crowd of 110,000 responds again with, "Sieg Heil! Sieg Heil! Sieg Heil!"

Americans shake their heads as Hitler continues speaking.

Lubin says, "I can't believe this."

"They treat him like a God or something," Joe responds.

Then Hitler announces, "Let the games begin!"

At that moment, by the east gate of the stadium, trumpeters lead another fanfare composed and conducted by Strauss as he debuts his classic *Olympic Hymn*. The white five-ringed Olympic flag rises as the Adonis runner stands on his toes to light the enormous caldron.

He holds the flaming torch up high and is silhouetted with partial clouds in the background. The enormous bell tolls and a chorus of thousands in white robes belt out Handel's "Hallelujah Chorus." As the sun sets, soft clouds whiff by and the stadium is filled with majesty.

Outside the stadium, reporters rush to their teletypes.

One English reporter says, "No doubt, Germany gets the gold for pageantry. The stage is set. Now, everyone has to do their best." Joe and the rest of the basketball team overhear this and walk in silence toward their bus. No more horsing around.

CHAPTER 28

HITLER AND JESSE OWENS

Inside the Olympic stadium, the green grass is perfectly manicured and the tracks are immaculate. The electric signage reflects the latest technology of the day, and the announcements are in German. Hope and anxiety fill the air. Runners warm up. Trainers hand out towels and blankets. Athletes sit on the grass and await their turn to compete.

An English-speaking journalist reports, "It's August 3 and the first day of the 1936 Olympics. A fine, sunny day in Berlin, Germany. It's not too hot and an exquisite day for track and field. Next up is the 100-meter race and the broad jump."

Athletes with the day off are packed in the stands and wear their country's Opening Ceremony outfits. Hitler beams with pride in his shaded box seat. Goebbels cheers, shakes hands, and accepts his well-deserved acknowledgements.

A relaxed Jesse Owens warms up in a white jersey and trunks. His spotless white track shoes seem to sparkle. Meticulously, Jesse lines up with the others for the 100-meters. He digs in for a flawless race. His body is primed and ready to spring into action. The starting gun goes off and Jesse takes the lead. Hitler and Goebbels root for Germany. The Gestapo in the stands make sure all the Germans are cheering. Brundage, Naismith, and the basketball players, including

Art Mollner, Gene Johnson, and Needles, cheer on Jesse Owens. When Jesse wins, the Americans howl.

Art Mollner comments, "So effortless. Like he was rocking in a chair."

Hitler and Goebbels are horrified and leave. Hitler bumps into a foreign photographer who asks, "Could I have your photo with Jesse Owens, sir?"

Aghast, Hitler angrily replies, "Do you really think I will allow myself to shake hands and be photographed with a Negro? White humanity should be ashamed of itself." Then Hitler storms off.

The next day, it's time for Jesse Owens to prove himself in the broad jump. Hitler cheers with the crowd as blonde German Lutz Long makes a spectacular jump. Jesse botches his jump and the basketball team and the rest of the Americans chant, "U.S.A. U.S.A. U.S.A."

After much suspense, Jesse beats Lutz for the gold. The Americans go crazy. Hitler and Goebbels leave again. Lutz throws his arm around Jesse and walks with him around the track. Officials frown as the crowd applauds politely. Later, the crowd watches as Jesse wins a third gold medal, for the 200-meter race.

Furious, Hitler paces in his office. Goebbels looks on and does his best to calm Hitler down.

"It's unfair to have people like Jesse Owens," Goebbels says. "You might as well have a deer or gazelle on your team."

Hitler angrily thumbs through various newspapers and reads aloud headlines that say "A Hole in Aryan Superiority" and "Jesse Owens—The World's Most Famous Athlete." He throws the papers across the room like a petulant child.

Meanwhile, at the stadium, Brundage tries to sneak by a group of reporters, but to no avail. "Your comments on Jesse Owens, sir," one asks.

"No nation since Greece has captured the Olympic spirit as has Germany," Brundage says diplomatically.

"You didn't answer my question."

Brundage, seething with anger, repeats himself as he bolts for a meeting. "No nation since Greece has captured the Olympic spirit as has Germany. Thank you."

CHAPTER 29

DOWN TO BUSINESS

The next day at their assigned converted "basketball court," a basketball practice is in progress. Needles hands Gene the final rules and paperwork. Skimming the papers, Gene motions for the team to huddle.

"Okay, boys, here's the last set of 'official' rules. No matter what, all men will play. Balter and Mollner, you too! We're not going to let a thug like Hitler tell us 'No Jews.'" The team cheers and slaps each other on the back.

Gene resumes, "They're being strict about the only-seven-can-suit-up-per-game rule, so no more than two of you can foul out. The rest of us will be in the stands cheering."

Needles adds, "We'll alternate you players. So, the opposition won't know what to expect."

Gene says, "There's seven games, so both teams will play three times. In the final game, an attempt will be made to find the strongest combination."

"We have six rounds with one day off. There's no seeding. We've got 23 countries with a single elimination."

"So, you have to be lucky every time. A 40-minute game clock with 60 minutes allowed for each game."

"Think soccer when it comes to fouls," Needles reminds. "Physical touching is a foul. The refs are all European, so we have to play the game their way."

Gene says, "They're unpaid, so there's no consequence if they make a mistake. So, you can't make any."

When word got around to the basketball community that Dr. James Naismith, the inventor of basketball would be attending the games, a fitting tribute was organized. In Olympic Opening Ceremony style, 199 players from 23 countries dip their flags to Naismith as they parade by him. With tears of joy, he is finally able to receive the love that people had been trying to bestow on him for the past 45 years.

The original eighteen Incorrigibles directly influenced seventeen of the national teams among the twenty-three countries parading before him. Joyfully, he claps and waves and thoroughly lives in the moment. He did it. He did something to make the world a better place. His heart is full of worldwide love and gratitude to those who embraced the game. The only thing missing is Maude. Oh, how he wished she were there.

On August 7, the first day of basketball, the U.S.A. has a bye. However, that does not stop Brundage, Van Ritter, and I.A. O'shaughnessy, along with families, friends, and fans, to bunch up on the crowded benches. Brundage notices that Hitler and other ranking officials are not present.

The first basketball game ever played in the Olympics occurs between Estonia and France. As the teams warm up, Naismith takes a moment alone to pray. After his prayer, he pulls out John McLendon's 50-cent piece from his pocket and rubs it between his fingers. Then he says to it, "We'll take all the luck we can get. Thank you." Then he heads to the game.

★ ★ ★

Naismith full of pride, stands center court and announces, "As I toss up the first ball, in the first basketball game played in the Olympics, I want to acknowledge the common diversity of the Olympics. We may not speak the same languages or have the same customs, but we have the common bond of basketball." The crowd cheers. Naismith steps in and tosses up the ball. There is a huge roar from the crowd.

★　★　★

The next day, the U.S.A. plays Estonia. Seven Americans (Gibbons, Smitty, Lubin, Shy, Knowles, Balter, Mollner) are suited up and ready to win. The other seven are in their dress suits beside Needles and Gene Johnson in the huddle.

Gene says, "Team U.S.A.! What an accomplishment to be here. I want all of you to know how much I respect your sacrifice and hard work. Whatever happens, we've made history."

Needles gets down to facts and reminds them, "Estonia is the European champ, and remember, the refs are European. Play by their rules. Prove to them that we can win, no matter what changes they throw at us." Needles extends his hand for hands in. The team joins him in saying, "Let's go get 'em!"

The confident Estonians have their own plodding game plan. The Americans take full advantage and attack. The tall combo of Smitty and Lubin annihilate Estonia's chance to win. Smitty scores 8, Lubin 13, Shy 10, and the U.S. spanks Estonia 52-28.

After a full day of basketball events, the Olympic athletic office is packed with angry and upset basketball competitors. Brundage; Needles; Gene Johnson; team captain Bill Wheatley; two European referees; the Peruvian coach, who is under five feet tall; and various reporters all vie for attention.

The Estonian referee explains, "It is considered undignified for Estonia to attack."

Gene argues, "You are mocking the North American under-standing of the game. These are completely different rules."

Bill interjects, "We don't know what's being called against us."

"To the Swiss refs, any foot movement is 'Progress,'" Needles adds.

In a huff, the Peruvian coach stomps out during the mass confusion. A reporter stops him and asks, "Why are you leaving?"

The Peruvian coach answers, "The umpires are giving bad calls and no one should play over 6'2"."

Gene overhears this and yells, "Objection!"

Needles quickly interjects, "There should be no height limit to basketball."

Brundage has heard enough and takes command. "All teams are staying, both tall and short. We'll alternate the referees. Understand that basketball is a minor sport to the Germans. Do your best with what they have given us."

The group grumbles and disperses.

Headlines in *The New York Times* August 11, 1936, read "Spain Called Home for Civil War" and "U.S. Basketball Advances to Quarterfinals."

August 12 is the quarterfinal: U.S.A. vs. Philippines. The Refiners along with Ralph Bishop practice somberly in their warm-up suits, adjusting to the way the light balloon ball is caught by the wind. Gene blows his whistle and says, "Let's go; suit up." The team hustles to the locker room.

When they arrive, the room is in complete disarray. The boys dash to their lockers: their jerseys are gone!

Joe shouts, "We have pants but no jerseys."

Needles yells, "They've stolen our jerseys?!"

Practical Bill asks, "What are we going to play in?"

Gene calls, "Let this fire you up. Find something else to wear and go win."

The boys improvise and enter the game with wrinkled T-shirts, looking and feeling like a rag-tag team. The crowd laughs. Naismith and the rest of the team on the bench are stoic.

Naismith says, "They can win without jerseys." The fans chant, "U.S.A. U.S.A. U.S.A."

Despite the outfits, the team plays cool, calm, and collected 1-on-1 basketball, forcing the Filipinos to run hard. At the half, the U.S. is only three points ahead. The team huddles.

Gene asks, "Ready to claim the quarterfinals?"

The team unanimously yells, "Yes!"

Bill orders, "Let's go get 'em!"

With that, the U.S. team charges the court. It's fire-alarm, harem-scarem, zone press at its finest. Joe scores 21 points, Francis 18. The Filipinos are so intimidated that they add only 3 points. Final score: U.S.A. 56, Philippines 23.

The next day, Thursday, August 13, 1936, is the semifinals game. Whoever wins goes on to play Canada. Whoever loses, gets the bronze medal. The Americans want only a gold medal and are mentally prepared for a tough match. In this game it's the U.S.A. vs. Mexico, and ironically, it's raining! Reporters and fans sit on the drenched outdoor benches. They all have umbrellas and bundle together to try to stay warm.

Gene paces on the sidelines and says, "Not again. My worst nightmare. Mexico in the rain! Be alert, boys. They might try something tricky."

No need to worry. The man-to-man Universals dominate the game, and Balter scores as many as the entire Mexican team. Lubin makes 9. At the half: U.S.A. 13, 2 easily. By the end of the game, it's a sea of mud, full of 10-foot skids. Final score: U.S.A. 25, Mexico 10.

Daley reports, "And Mexico wins the bronze. The United States and Canada advance to finals to see who wins the gold."

The U.S. and Mexican teams congratulate each other, hurrying out of the rain.

Back in Kansas, in a corner booth at the Echo Café, Phog surrounds himself with sports pages of top newspapers. He listens to the radio and smiles to himself as the U.S. advances. Fans stop by his booth to congratulate him.

At the Naismith home, Maude is feeling better and is surrounded by reporters, family, and well-wishers. They listen to the game, clip articles, and make scrapbooks.

John McLendon has congregated his black youth teams at a Kansas University rec room. They listen to the basketball games on the radio and cheer at every U.S. point.

★   ★   ★

Now it's August 14. The day of the final game: U.S.A. vs. Canada. It's pouring rain and 50 degrees outside. Reporters in raincoats await the arrival of Needles and Gene Johnson. Needles takes a moment for Daley, the *Times* reporter.

Daley asks, "There seems to be a dominance of American basketball. Any comment?"

Needles answers, "Any good Midwestern high school team could defeat any team in the tournament with the exception of the U.S., Canada, Japan, Mexico, and the Philippines."

Overhearing this, Gene grabs Needles' arm and ushers him away.

Gene says to the reporters, "Needles is more of a manager than a coach. Thank you, Gentlemen." Gene maneuvers Needles away from the spotlight.

"Hey, leave me alone," Needles demands as he pulls away from Gene's grip.

"Shut your trap," Gene says forcefully. "We haven't won yet and we don't want to rile Canada."

Now, Needles is anxious to change the subject and says, "We gotta' move the finals inside. Here's the latest Canadian report." Gene takes the Canadian player report and sees Doug Peden's name marked in red.

Gene says, "Peden. 19 points in the semifinals. Ian Allison, a top scorer. And the Chapman brothers. Got it!"

Needles and Gene arrive at the Olympic athletic office. Gordie Fuller, the Canadian coach, catches up with them. Brundage joins the group along with two German officials.

Fuller threatens, "We can't play in this rain."

The German official simply laughs and says, "Of course you can. Just like soccer or rugby."

"Rainy weather will make it a more exciting game," adds the second German official.

Gene reminds the group, "It's not designed to be played in the rain. It's an indoor game."

Needles suggests, "It would be easy to set up an indoor venue. All you need are uprights and court markings."

Brundage gently steps forward and confronts the officials, saying, "They deserve a decent court."

The second German official says, "We have been saving court number 4 for the finals. It was covered earlier, before the rain intensified."

Gene tries not to panic and logically informs the group, "Now our tip-off is delayed. It's 25 minutes closer to dark."

The German official is adamant. "As planned, the final game will be played on court number 4. We'll make adjustments as needed."

At the court, several hundred fans have assembled in the rain to see the finals. German officials huddle with umbrellas. The savvy Canadians wear Hudson Bay parkas and have umbrellas as well. There is a special stand for Hitler and his dignitaries; however, Hitler isn't there.

A Canadian asks a German official, "Where's Hitler?"

"It does not rain on the Fuhrer," the German official answers.

The Canadian laughs and says, "He's just angry because the U.S. beat the Germans in rowing."

"I'll have you know, Germany has won the most gold medals and the most medals overall. Why should our Fuhrer trouble himself in the rain?" The German official moves on and leaves the Canadian steaming mad.

Now, it's still raining and almost night. The selected team (Ralph Bishop, Joe Fortenberry, Francis Johnson, Carl Knowles, Jack Ragland, Carl Shy, and Bill Wheatley) is led by Joe and Bill. They wear cape-style raincoats and do their best to keep their shoes dry. As they walk several blocks to the court, it seems that the rain is getting worse. Reporters hurriedly tag after them, adding to the splish-splash. When the players arrive at the decorative sunken court, they grimace when they see that even though the court was covered, there's four inches of standing water.

Workers carefully remove the tarp, and the game begins briskly and unceremoniously. The officials, players, and fans just want to get this game over with.

In the first half, Canada's Ian Allison scores the first three points. The U.S. is caught off guard and doesn't like it. Adding to the misery, the slippery ball absorbs water in the slosh and changes weight between too light and too heavy. The referees do their best to keep dry balls in play and exchange them often. The American team seems a bit bewildered. Gene calls time out and the team huddles.

Francis says, "The ball is impossible to handle and it's slick as hell out there."

Gene lashes out, "Lack of accuracy will defeat this tough team. Peden can be controlled. Bill, stay on him."

"Like a bulldog. I won't let him go," Bill promises.

"They're stockier and shorter. Joe, block their shots," Gene orders.

Joe nods and the team returns to the court. Francis floats the ball to Jack. Bill dogs the fast-shooting Peden, hounds him relentlessly, and routinely shuts down his inside shots. Not taking any chances, Joe stays back as rover and makes eight points. There's no pivoting due to mud, and everyone is skidding, disoriented, and mud soaked. The lime-drawn lines are covered with six inches of standing mud, completely stopping Canada's speed and patterned defense. The Refiners revise accordingly; Ragland scores four and Wheatley nets three.

A referee blows his whistle and says, "No 3-point baskets. The clock will be continuous due to darkness."

Determined, Joe leaps up and catches balls headed for the net. He bats away every jump ball. Daley sits in the stands with Balter and the rest of the team. He says, "Joe Fortenberry is the first 'big man' in basketball. He gets the tip and he's always there. Best center in the world."

"The best," Balter agrees.

A referee blows his whistle for the shortened halftime. America leads 15-4. Workers cover the court. The team huddles.

Gene says, "All we have to do now is stop the ball. Let the clock win this one for us. The team nods to each other and heads toward the court to get that gold medal win.

Again, the tarp covering the court is pulled for the second half. It's obvious that the court is just as soaked as before. Reporters, Naismith, the rest of the team, and the crowd hold their breath as the ball slips through the players' hands. They have some hysterically funny moments as the players slosh in the sea of mud. Ian Allison, Canada's top scorer in the first half, can't get around Joe. 6'3" Art Chapman and 6'2" Chuck Chapman have run out of steam and lost their edge.

Balter and the others chuckle, "None of the players are recognizable."

"This is a thousand laughs," Needles comments.

Gene yells to the team, "Just be careful."

Daley reports, "Jack Ragland, the highlight of the second half, just lands on the ball and stays there."

Needles says, "It's really … now it's just muddy chaos. It's so slippery, they look like greased pigs. The Berg ball is absorbing water like a sponge."

With only four points made in the second half, Canada makes a final rush toward the basket. Bill Wheatley is there to stop Peden, and Joe leaps up and bats the ball to Ragland. With athletic precision, he falls on the ball and holds on tight to run out the clock. The U.S.A.

wins 19 to 8! The soaked fans cheer. Daley rushes to an overjoyed Naismith and says, "America wins the gold! And Canada goes home with the silver. Congratulations, Dr. Naismith!"

"This is the happiest moment of my life! I can't believe it."

Canadian Jim Stewart trots to his wife on the sidelines, gives her a hug, and sticks a game ball under her coat as they leave. Even in the rain, people push to congratulate Naismith and the U.S. team.

In the Olympic stadium on Sunday, August 16, the closing medal ceremony is under way. It's the kind of God-given sunny day that glistens after a rain. Naismith stands on the gold medal awards podium. The basketball team lines up, starting with team captain Bill Wheatley followed by Joe, and the rest of the squad. A German announcer introduces the basketball medalists, ending with the Americans.

When Naismith hears the announcement, he holds the medal for a moment, as if saying a silent prayer of gratitude. Then he presents the first Olympic gold medal in basketball to Bill Wheatley, as Joe and the rest of the team surround them. "The Star-Spangled Banner" plays in the background, while Naismith and basketball's first Olympic gold medal team place their hands over their hearts and stare at the American flag with tears in their eyes.

CHAPTER 30

HOME

Back home in Kansas, Naismith is treated like a rock star of today. By now, he's used to it. He's been in the New York City ticker-tape parade, met dozens of dignitaries, and socialized with high society. But this time he's home, and the familiar faces in the crowd like John McLendon's warm his heart. He can't wait to see Maude and tell her about his adventure.

As usual, reporters and others surround him. John recognizes this and quickly grabs Naismith's luggage and steers him toward the car. What Naismith needs is a little peace and time with Maude, not all this fanfare. They drive along Naismith's favorite route and pass by homes, schools, and playgrounds with basketball hoops. John steers the car to the front of the Naismith house. Naismith gets out and takes a moment to breathe in the Kansas air. John helps him with his luggage.

"Thank you, John. It's good to be home again."

John says, "Congratulations, sir." Then he starts to go.

Naismith stops him and says, "Wait! I have something for you." He dips into his pocket and pulls out the fifty-cent piece. "Take this. I hope it brings you as much luck as it brought me." Smiling from ear to ear, John takes the coin, puts it in his pocket, and says, "Thank you, sir. I hope so, too." They shake hands, back-slap, and say good-bye.

As Naismith opens the front door, Maude steps out of the bedroom in a sheer cotton nightie.

"Welcome home, Champ," she purrs.

"Dearie, I have so much to tell you," he says with tears in his eyes.

They lovingly hug, kiss, and stroll toward to the bedroom.

EPILOGUE

At the Basketball Hall of Fame, John McLendon finishes his induction speech. "In closing, I want to thank Dr. James Naismith for his leadership and his gift to the world." The audience starts to applaud, then John reaches into his pocket and pulls out the 50-cent piece and shows it to the crowd and says, "Basketball was certainly a gift to me. Mind, body, spirit!" The crowd enthusiastically rises to give John a standing ovation.

★ ★ ★

The 1936 first Olympic gold medal team has been nominated for induction into the Naismith Memorial Basketball Hall of Fame.

★ ★ ★

Today over 450,000,000 people play basketball worldwide.

WHATEVER HAPPENED TO...

JAMES NAISMITH (1861–1939). The inventor and father of basketball. The Naismith Memorial Basketball Hall of Fame in Springfield, Massachusetts, is named for him. He never patented his invention and never made royalties.

MAUDE SHERMAN NAISMITH (1870–1937). She organized the first women's basketball team and designed the first football helmet. Although deaf since her second pregnancy, she was an advocate for social issues and basketball.

PHOG ALLEN (1885–1974). The father of basketball coaching. He had 746 career wins and was the main force in getting basketball into the Olympics. He understood the basketball business and made money from endorsements and clinics.

JOHN McLENDON JR. (1915–1999). A hall-of-famer for being the father of basketball integration and a legendary coach. He arranged the first integrated game with Duke in 1944 and won! His coaching career spanned seven decades. He is one of the most respected figures in basketball.

EARNEST "QUIG" QUIGLEY, (1880–1960). He was the basketball head referee for the American Olympic Trials in 1936 and was inducted into the Basketball Hall of Fame in 1961. He umpired over 3,000 major league baseball games.

★ ★ ★

TEAM U.S.A—THE FIRST BASKETBALL OLYMPIC GOLD
MEDALISTS

COACH JIMMY NEEDLES (1900–1969). The first U.S. head basketball coach. He brought home the gold! From Loyola Marymount,
he produced two Hall of Famers, Phil Woolpert and Pete Newell.
He coached the great Saint Ignatius squads in the 1950s.

COACH GENE JOHNSON (1902–1989). The father of modern basketball. He pioneered many dynamic basketball changes, including
the fast break, the full-court zone press, the slam dunk, and
goal tending (no longer allowed). He made more money selling
insurance.

SAM BALTER (1909–1998). One of six Jews on the 1936 U.S. Olympic
Team. He pioneered sports telecasting in Southern California
and was inducted to the Helms Sports Hall of Fame and received
a Golden Mike Award for Sports Broadcasting. Playing in the
1936 Olympics was the "highlight of his life."

RALPH BISHOP (1915–1974). From the University of Washington,
he was the final player chosen, and at age 20, also the youngest.
He played in three matches, including the last game. He won the
U.S. Olympians ping-pong match on the *S.S. Manhattan*.

JOE FORTENBERRY (1911–1993). He invented the slam dunk and
was Basketball's first "big man." He's in the Helms Sports Hall
of Fame and Texas Panhandle Hall of Fame. A four-time A.A.U.
All American, he worked at Phillips Oil 28 years.

JOHN "TEX" GIBBONS (1907–1984). He was from Stratford, Texas,
and at age 28 was one of the oldest players on the team. He
taught and coached at U.C.L.A. and went on to a long career at
Phillips Oil.

FRANCIS JOHNSON (1910–1997). A ball hawk known for his steals.
He shot with either hand and had keen hand-to-eye coordina-
tion. Quite the horseman, he was inducted into the Appaloosa
Horse Hall of Fame in 1988.

FRANK LUBIN (1910–1999). The father of Lithuanian basketball was a longtime motivator and spoke internationally long after his service in World War II. He was a grip at Twentieth Century Fox and retired in 1967.

ART MOLLNER (1912–1995). He won the 1941 A.A.U. National Championship for Twentieth Century Fox along with Olympians Frank Lubin, Carl Knowles, and Carl Shy. He loved police work and retired as a plain-clothes detective after 31 years.

JACK RAGLAND (1913–1996). A Kansan from Wichita State, he was one of the originals with Coach Gene Johnson. He played in three Olympic games, landing on the ball to run out the clock in the final game. He became an attorney with Phillips Oil.

WILLARD "SMITTY" SCHMIDT (1910–1965). He got rheumatic fever while playing for the Antlers Hotel in Colorado. Hospitalized for 6 weeks, his playing days were over. He briefly coached basketball, excelled in bridge, and enjoyed his family life.

BILL WHEATLEY (1909–1992). The first unofficial A.A.U. historian. He conducted basketball clinics around the world for the State Department and mentored Don Barksdale, who became the first African-American on an Olympic Basketball team in 1948.

As for the SILVER MEDALISTS, 1936 was the only year that Canada has medaled in basketball. Jim Stewart's son still has the Berg ball from that last game. It's a prized family possession.

BIBLIOGRAPHY

Books:

Brown, Daniel James. 2013. *The Boys in the Boat.*

Cohen, Stan. 1996. *The Games of '36—A Pictorial History of the 1936 Olympics in Germany.*

Doherty, Thomas. 2013. *Hollywood and Hitler 1933–1939.*

Hennes, Doug. 2014. *The Great Heart—The Life of I. A. O'shaughnessy: Oilman and Philanthropist.*

Hillenbrand, Laura. 2010. *Unbroken.*

Hughes, Rich. 2011. *Netting Out Basketball 1936—The Remarkable Story of the McPherson Refiners, the First Team to Dunk, Zone Press and Win the Olympic Gold Medal.*

Jackson, Phil, with Hugh Delehanty. 2013. *Eleven Rings: The Soul of Success.*

Johnson, Scott Morrow. 2016. *Phog—The Most Influential Man in Basketball.*

Kahn, Barbara Balter. 2010. *Sam Balter—His Life and Times.*

Katz, Milton S. 2007. *Breaking Through—John B. McLendon: Basketball Legend and Civil Rights Pioneer.*

Kerkoff, Blair. 1996. *Phog Allen—The Father of Basketball Coaching.*

Large, David Clay. 2007. *Nazi Games—The Olympics of 1936.*

Mandell, Richard D. 1971. *The Nazi Olympics.*

Naismith, James. 1941. *Basketball: It's Origin and Development.*

Phelps, Richard "Digger," with John Walters and Tim Bourret. 2001. *Basketball for Dummies.*

Rains, Rob, with Hellen Carpenter. 2009. *James Naismith—The Man Who Invented Basketball.*

Sports Illustrated Kids. 2014. *Slam Dunk! Top 10 Lists of Everything in Basketball.*

Urwand, Ben. 2013. *The Collaboration—Hollywood's Past with Hitler.*

Articles:

Amarillo Globe News

The Denver Post

Kansas Alcoholic Beverage Control

The New York Times

Sports Illustrated

Wikipedia

Y.M.C.A National History

Archives:

21st Century Fox Archives. Jeff Thompson

McPherson Convention Center. Ann Hassler

McPherson Museum. Brett Whitenack

Naismith Memorial Basketball Hall of Fame Archives. Jeff Zeysing

Universal Studios Archives. Jeff Pirtle

Interviews:

Jon Mark Beilue, Barbara "Bobbie" Fortenberry, Oliver Fortenberry, Sally Fortenberry Nibbelink, Trish Fortenberry Hill, Jerry Johnson, Connie Schweer, Ed Wright

Videos:

100 Years of Kansas Basketball, YouTube

Berlin Olympics—Canadian Team Training Traveling and Competing 1936, Chapman Bros. Home Video

The Boys of '36—The S.S. Manhatttan, American Experience, PBS

The Dust Bowl—Ken Burns, PBS

Jesse Owens—American Experience, PBS

Oil and Gold—The McPherson Globe Refiners Basketball Story, McPherson CVB Film

Olympia—The Complete Version, Leni Riefenstahl, Pathfinder Home Entertainment

Race—The Incredible True Story of Gold Medal Champion Jesse Owens, Forecast Pictures

S.S. Manhattan *Interior*, YouTube

Triumph of the Will, Leni Riefenstahl, Synapse Films

The Wonderful, Horrible Life of Leni Riefenstahl, Kino Video

Recordings:

Chuck Chapman, Doug Peden Interview, 1975

The Globe Refiners—Tallest Team in the World Reunions, 1972, 1986, 2006

Naismith Rare Recordings, 1939—YouTube

ABOUT THE AUTHOR

Beth Fortenberry is an award-winning writer/
producer in Los Angeles. She got her Actors
Equity card when she was 19 and her Screen
Actors Guild card at 21. To make ends meet,
she worked as a Playboy Bunny in New York.
She's a member of the Academy of Television
Arts and Sciences and faithfully votes for the
Emmys. She and her husband are Newlywed
champs and went on to be Goldywed champs twice! They are living
happily, even after 30 years of marriage. She has two children,
a stepson, a grandson, and a miniature Yorkie. She loves her life,
ballroom dancing, and sports!

9 781948 181914